Penguin Modern Poets
VOLUME 7

Donald Davie, a Fellow of the British Academy and for forty years a poet and translator, was educated in Barnsley and at Cambridge University. His academic career continued through various English, Irish and American universities, where he taught literary history and verse-writing. He chiefly concerned himself with poetry in English from the eighteenth and twentieth centuries, though he also wrote on Slavic literature. He served with the Royal Navy during the Second World War in Russia and India. He was an Honorary Fellow of St Catharine's College, Cambridge, and of Trinity College, Dublin. He edited *The New Oxford Book of Christian Verse* and *The Psalms in English* for the Penguin Classics series. Donald Davie died in September 1995.

Samuel Menashe was born in New York City in 1925. In 1943 he enlisted and was sent to the Infantry School in Fort Benning, Georgia. He was stationed in England before entering combat in France. In 1950 he was awarded a *doctorat d'université* by the Sorbonne. His first book, *The Many Named Beloved*, was published in London in 1961, thanks to Kathleen Raine, who wrote the foreword. It was followed by *No Jerusalem But This*, *Fringe of Fire*, *To Open* and *Collected Poems*. In 1957 he received a Longview Foundation Award for a war story and a group of poems.

Allen Curnow was born in 1911 at Timaru, New Zealand. He was educated at the universities of Canterbury and Auckland, and in 1951 he joined the English Department at the University of Auckland, where he taught until 1976. His first book of poems appeared in 1933, and his many published works include *Collected Poems* (1974) and *Continuum: New and Later Poems 1973–1989*, as well as plays, a book of criticism and anthologies. He was awarded a CBE in 1986, and has received the New Zealand Book Award for poetry six times, the Dillons Commonwealth Poetry Prize for 1988, the Queen's Gold Medal for Poetry in 1989, the Order of New Zealand in 1990 and the Cholmondeley Award for Poets in 1992.

The Penguin Modern Poets Series

Penguin Modern Poets

VOLUME 7

DONALD DAVIE

SAMUEL MENASHE

ALLEN CURNOW

PENGUIN BOOKS

Published by the Penguin Group
Penguin Books Ltd, 27 Wrights Lane, London w8 5tz, England
Penguin Books USA Inc., 375 Hudson Street, New York, New York 10014, USA
Penguin Books Australia Ltd, Ringwood, Victoria, Australia
Penguin Books Canada Ltd, 10 Alcorn Avenue, Toronto, Ontario, Canada m4v 3b2
Penguin Books (NZ) Ltd, 182–190 Wairau Road, Auckland 10, New Zealand

Penguin Books Ltd, Registered Offices: Harmondsworth, Middlesex, England

This selection first published 1996
10 9 8 7 6 5 4 3 2 1

Set in 10.75/13pt Monotype Garamond
Typeset by Datix International Limited, Bungay, Suffolk
Printed in England by Clays Ltd, St Ives plc

Contents

Allen Curnow

Donald Davie

At Knaresborough

'Broad acres, sir.' You hear them in my talk.
As tell-tale as a pigment in the skin,
Vowels as broad as all the plain of York
Proclaim me of this country and your kin.

And, gratified to have your guess endorsed,
You warm to me. I thaw, and am approved.
But, to be frank, the sentiment is forced,
When I pretend, for your sake, to be moved.

To feel so little, when his sympathies
Would be so much engaged (he would have said),
Surprised the poet too. But there it is,
The heart is not to be solicited.

Believe me, sir, I only ply my trade,
Which is to know when I am played upon.
You might have moved, you never shall persuade.
You grow too warm. I must be moving on.

Poem as Abstract

'To write about a tree . . . you must first *be* a tree.'

                      – W. R. Rodgers

I

A poem is less an orange than a grid;
It hoists a charge; it does not ooze a juice.
It has no rind, being entirely hard.

All drumming yards and open, it asserts
That clouds have way upon them, and that hills
Breast into time behind a singing strut.

A sheer abstraction, apt upon the grass
Of London parks, has emulated oak
And aped the ramage that it could surpass.

That construct, ribbed with wire across a quern,
Is caging such serenity of stress
As boughs, or fruit that breaks them, cannot learn.

For gods are gathered from the styles they wear,
And do they curl, a foetus in a fruit,
Or, like Orion, pinned upon the air?

II

No trowelled matron but a rigger's mate,
The pile-high poet has no time to brood.
He steps the mast; it does not germinate.

Not for ingestion but to frame the air
He flies the spar that even winter's tree
In green ambition cannot grow so spare.

The orange dangles, drops, and comes again.
To make a fruit he has to be a fruit,
A globe of pulp about a pip of pain.

But tip-toe cages lofted in a day
(To make a grid he has to *make* a grid)
Have come unprecedented, and to stay.

If poems make a style, a way of walking
With enterprise, should not a poet's gait
Be counties-wide, this stride, the pylons stalking?

Belfast on a Sunday Afternoon

Visiting Belfast at the end of June,
We found the Orange Lodge behind a band:
Sashes and bearskins in the afternoon,
White cotton gloves upon a crippled hand.

Pastmasters pale, elaborately grim,
Marched each alone, beneath a bowler hat:
And, catapulted on a crumpled limb,
A lame man leapt the tram-lines like a bat.

And first of all we tried to laugh it off,
Acting bemusement in the grimy sun;
But stayed to worry where we came to scoff,
As loud contingents followed, one by one.

Pipe bands, flute bands, brass bands and silver bands,
Presbyter's pibroch and the deacon's serge,
Came stamping where the iron Maenad stands,
Victoria, glum upon a grassy verge.

Some brawny striplings sprawled upon the lawn;
No man is really crippled by his hates.
Yet I remembered with a sudden scorn
Those 'passionate intensities' of Yeats.

Pushkin. A Didactic Poem

... he did not yet know well those hidden mechanisms of the person by which it achieves its isolation from others and withdraws into itself; he was entirely surrendered to his genius, disarmed by his own power; and if his pride led him to challenge God, he cancelled by that very act his own right to deny Him.

– Wladimir Weidlé

What with hounds and friends and, in the winter,
Skating, he was seldom bored.
He had learned to be wary, was at pains, I think,
To remain amused?

In the matter of Pushkin, Emily Brontë
Is the best analogy in some ways
Among our poets. As in her verse,
In Pushkin's we assume the truth
That for life to be tolerable, man must
Be wary, ingenious, quick to change
Among diversions, grave or frivolous,
To keep off spleen; although for her,
As she was a woman, a narrower range
Presented itself, and so she is less
Various, flexible, fiery, though as noble
As Pushkin was, more stoical.

Pushkin's draughts-playing and his drinking,
His friends, his travelling, even some
Of his mistresses, he considered as
So many improvisations against
Boredom. But the boredom was
No vacancy nor want of occupation
Nor lack of resources. It was the spleen,

And Pushkin certainly fled before it
Or circumvented it. His poems
Record the circumventions as
Hours when the mind, turned outwards, knew
Friendships or the approach of death
As gifts. The poet exhibits here
How to be conscious in every direction
But that of the self, where deception starts.
This is nobility; not lost
Wholly perhaps, if lost to art.

Grateful tears, delicious sorrow,
Said the Russian gentleman,
Mozart will be dead tomorrow
Of this confusion.

As Byron said of Keats, 'I don't
mean he is indecent, but
viciously soliciting
his own ideas.'

(Schiller and Dostoievsky, oysters
Pearling their own disease, the saints
Full of self-help)

Long before Shakespeare wrote, or Donne,
In the modern manner, there were minds
Aware of themselves, and figuring this
In psychomachia. But the Greeks
Knew states of innocence, the will
Turned always outwards, courage the gift
Counting for virtue, and control,
As of the craven self, a notion
Lost in the social usage. Thus

Self-consciousness is not at fault
In itself. It can be kept
Other than morbid, under laws
Of disciplined sensibility, such
As the seventeenth-century Wit.
But all such disciplines depend
On disciplines of social use,
Now widely lost. Yet there are those
Few men remaining, gifted, or
Especially heroic, or,
Like Pushkin, brilliantly both.
Ask when we are diseased, and these
Will answer: When the moral will
Intervenes to sap the heart,
When the difficult feelings are
Titillated and confused
For novel combinations, or
Ransacked for virtue.

Remains the voice that moves on silence
In moral commonplace, where yet
Some thwart and stern communal sense
Whispers, before we all forget.

What need dissection of the thrust
Which motivates the skating feet,
When that can always be deduced
From the figure of eight?

What need dissection of the thrust
Which motivates the skating feet?
Skating with friends in the winter,
He foretold our defeat.

Remembering the 'Thirties

I

Hearing one saga, we enact the next.
We please our elders when we sit enthralled;
But then they're puzzled; and at last they're vexed
To have their youth so avidly recalled.

It dawns upon the veterans after all
That what for them were agonies, for us
Are high-brow thrillers, though historical;
And all their feats quite strictly fabulous.

This novel written fifteen years ago,
Set in my boyhood and my boyhood home,
These poems about 'abandoned workings', show
Worlds more remote than Ithaca or Rome.

The Anschluss, Guernica – all the names
At which those poets thrilled or were afraid
For me mean schools and schoolmasters and games;
And in the process someone is betrayed.

Ourselves perhaps. The Devil for a joke
Might carve his own initials on our desk,
And yet we'd miss the point because he spoke
An idiom too dated, Audenesque.

Ralegh's Guiana also killed his son.
A pretty pickle if we came to see
The tallest story really packed a gun,
The Telemachiad an Odyssey.

II

Even to them the tales were not so true
As not to be ridiculous as well;
The ironmaster met his Waterloo,
But Rider Haggard rode along the fell.

'Leave for Cape Wrath tonight!' They lounged away
On Fleming's trek or Isherwood's ascent.
England expected every man that day
To show his motives were ambivalent.

They played the fool, not to appear as fools
In time's long glass. A deprecating air
Disarmed, they thought, the jeers of later schools;
Yet irony itself is doctrinaire,

And, curiously, nothing now betrays
Their type to time's derision like this coy
Insistence on the quizzical, their craze
For showing Hector was a mother's boy.

A neutral tone is nowadays preferred.
And yet it may be better, if we must,
To praise a stance impressive and absurd
Than not to see the hero for the dust.

For courage is the vegetable king,
The sprig of all ontologies, the weed
That beards the slag-heap with his hectoring,
Whose green adventure is to run to seed.

Time Passing, Beloved

Time passing, and the memories of love
Coming back to me, carissima, no more mockingly
Than ever before; time passing, unslackening,
Unhastening, steadily; and no more
Bitterly, beloved, the memories of love
Coming into the shore.

How will it end? Time passing and our passages of love
As ever, beloved, blind
As ever before; time binding, unbinding
About us; and yet to remember
Never less chastening, nor the flame of love
Less like an ember.

What will become of us? Time
Passing, beloved, and we in a sealed
Assurance unassailed
By memory. How can it end,
This siege of a shore that no misgivings have steeled,
No doubts defend?

Dream Forest

These have I set up,
Types of ideal virtue,
To be authenticated
By no one's Life and Times,
But by a sculptor's logic

Of whom I have commanded,
To dignify my groves,
Busts in the antique manner,
Each in the space mown down
Under its own sway:

First, or to break the circle,
Brutus, imperious, curbed
Not much by the general will,
But by a will to be curbed,
A preference for limits;

Pushkin next, protean
Who recognized no checks
Yet brooked them all – a mind
Molten and thereby fluent,
Unforced, easily strict;

The next, less fortunate,
Went honourably mad,
The angry annalist
Of hearth and marriage bed,
Strindberg – a staring head.

Classic, romantic, realist,
These have I set up.
These have I set, and a few trees.
When will a grove grow over
This mile upon mile of moor?

The Mushroom Gatherers

After Mickiewicz

Strange walkers! See their processional
Perambulations under low boughs,
The birches white, and the green turf under.
These should be ghosts by moonlight wandering.

Their attitudes strange: the human tree
Slowly revolves on its bole. All around
Downcast looks; and the direct dreamer
Treads out in trance his lane, unwavering.

Strange decorum: so prodigal of bows,
Yet lost in thought and self-absorbed, they meet
Impassively, without acknowledgement.
A courteous nation, but unsociable.

Field full of folk, in their immunity
From human ills, crestfallen and serene.
Who would have thought these shades our lively friends?
Surely these acres are Elysian Fields.

The Wind at Penistone

The wind meets me at Penistone.
                    A hill
Curves empty through the township, on a slope
Not cruel, and yet steep enough to be,
Were it protracted, cruel.
                    In the street,
A plain-ness rather meagre than severe,
Affords, though quite unclassical, a vista
So bald as to be monumental.
                    Here
A lean young housewife meets me with the glance
I like to think that I can recognize
As dour, not cross.
                    And all the while the wind,
A royal catspaw, toying easily,
Flicks out of shadows from a tufted wrist,
Its mane, perhaps, this lemon-coloured sun.

The wind reserves, the hill reserves, the style
Of building houses on the hill reserves
A latent edge;
                    which we can do without
In Pennine gradients and the Pennine wind,
And never miss, or, missing it, applaud
The absence of the aquiline;
                    which in her
Whose style of living in the wind reserves
An edge to meet the wind's edge, we may miss
But without prejudice.
                    And yet in art
Where all is patent, and a latency
Is manifest or nothing, even I,
Liking to think I feel these sympathies,
Can hardly praise this clenched and muffled style.

For architecture asks a cleaner edge,
Is open-handed.
                    And close-fisted people
Are mostly vulgar; only in the best,
Who draw, inflexible, upon reserves,
Is there a stern game that they play with life,
In which the rule is not to show one's hand
Until compelled.
                    And then the lion's paw!
Art that is dour and leonine in the Alps
Grows kittenish, makes curios and clocks,
Giant at play.
                    Here, nothing. So the wind
Meets me at Penistone, and, coming home,
The poet falls to special pleading, chilled
To find in Art no fellow but the wind.

The Wearing of the Green

Gold is not autumn's privilege;
A tawny ripening
In Meath in May burns ready in the hedge;
The yellow that will follow spring
Accentuates its wet and green array,
A sumptuous trill beneath
The shriller edge
Of Meath in May.

Green more entire must needs be evergreen,
Precluding autumn and this spring
Of Meath in May, its in-between
Of golds and yellows preluding

The liquid summer. Must the seasons stay
Their temperate career because
A flag is green
In Meath in May?

Imagination, Irish avatar,
Aches in the spring's heart and in mine, the stranger's,
In Meath in May. But to believe there are
Unchanging Springs endangers,
By that fast dye, the earth;
So blood-red green the season,
It never changes
In Meath in May.

A Winter Talent

Lighting a spill late in the afternoon,
I am that coal whose heat it should unfix;
Winter is come again; and none too soon
For meditation on its raft of sticks.

Some quick bright talents can dispense with coals
And burn their boats continually, command
An unreflecting brightness that unrolls
Out of whatever firings come to hand.

What though less sunny spirits never turn
The dry detritus of an August hill
To dangerous glory? Better still to burn
Upon that gloom where all have felt a chill.

Rejoinder to a Critic

You may be right: 'How can I dare to feel?'
May be the only question I can pose,
'And haply by abstruse research to steal
From my own nature all the natural man'
My sole resource. And I do not suppose
That others may not have a better plan.

And yet I'll quote again, and gloss it too
(You know by now my liking for collage):
Donne could be daring, but he never knew,
When he inquired, 'Who's injured by my love?'
Love's radio-active fall-out on a large
Expanse around the point it bursts above.

'Alas, alas, who's injured by my love?'
And recent history answers: Half Japan!
Not love, but hate? Well, both are versions of
The 'feeling' that you dare me to . . . Be dumb!
Appear concerned only to make it scan!
How dare we now be anything but numb?

To a Brother in the Mystery
Circa 1290

The world of God has turned its two stone faces
One my way, one yours. Yet we change places
A little, slowly. After we had halved
The work between us, those grotesques I carved
There in the first bays clockwise from the door,
That was such work as I got credit for

At York and Beverley: thorn-leaves twined and bent
To frame some small and human incident
Domestic or of venery. Each time I crossed
Since then, however, underneath the vast
Span of our Mansfield limestone, to appraise
How you cut stone, my emulous hard gaze
Has got to know you as I know the stone
Where none but chisels talk for us. I have grown
Of my own way of thinking yet of yours,
Seeing your leafage burgeon there by the doors
With a light that, flickering, trenches the voussoir's line;
Learning your pre-harmonies, design
Nourished by exuberance, and fine-drawn
Severity that is tenderness, I have thought,
Looking at these last stalls that I have wrought
This side of the chapter's octagon, I find
No hand but mine at work, yet mine refined
By yours, and all the difference: my motif
Of foliate form, your godliness in leaf.
  And your last spandrel proves the debt incurred
Not all on the one side. There I see a bird
Pecks at your grapes, and after him a fowler,
A boy with a bow. Elsewhere, your leaves discover
Of late blank mask-like faces. We infect
Each other then, doubtless to good effect . . .
And yet, take care: this cordial knack bereaves
The mind of all its sympathy with leaves,
Even with stone. I would not take away
From your peculiar mastery, if I say
A sort of coldness is the core of it,
A sort of cruelty; that prerequisite
Perhaps I rob you of, and in exchange give
What? Vulgarity's prerogative,
Indulgence towards the frailties it indulges,
Humour called 'wryness' that acknowledges

Its own complicity. I can keep in mind
So much at all events, can always find
Fallen humanity enough, in stone,
Yes, in the medium; where we cannot own
Crispness, compactness, elegance, but the feature
Seals it and signs it work of human nature
And fallen though redeemable. You, I fear,
Will find you bought humanity too dear
At the price of some light leaves, if you begin
To find your handling of them growing thin,
Insensitive, brittle. For the common touch,
Though it warms, coarsens. Never care so much
For leaves or people, but you care for stone
A little more. The medium is its own
Thing, and not all a medium, but the stuff
Of mountains; cruel, obdurate, and rough.

With the Grain

I

Why, by an ingrained habit, deviate
    Into their own ideas
Activities like carpentry, become
    The metaphors of graining?
Gardening, the one word, tilth? Or thought,
    The idea of having ideas,
Resolved into images of tilth and graining?

An ingrained habit . . . This is fanciful:
    And there's the rub
Bristling, where the irritable block

Screams underneath the blade
Of love's demand, or in crimped and gouged-out
    Shavings only, looses
Under a peeling logic its perceptions.

Language (mine, when wounding,
    Yours, back-biting) lacks
No whorl nor one-way shelving. It resists,
    Screams its remonstrance, planes
Reluctantly to a level. And the most
    Reasonable of settlements betrays
Unsmoothed resentment under the caress.

II

The purest hue, let only the light be sufficient
    Turns colour. And I was told
If painters frequent St Ives
    It is because the light
There, under the cliff, is merciful. I dream
    Of an equable light upon words
And as painters paint in St Ives, the poets speaking.

Under that cliff we should say, my dear,
    Not what we mean, but what
The words would mean. We should speak,
    As carpenters work,
With the grain of our words. We should utter
    Unceasingly the hue of love
Safe from the battery of changeable light.

(Love, a condition of such fixed colour,
    Cornwall indeed, or Wales
Might foster. Lovers in mauve,

Like white-robed Druids
Or the Bards in blue, would need
    A magical philtre, no less,
Like Iseult's, to change partners.)

III

Such a fourth estate of the realm,
    Hieratic unwinking
Mauve or blue under skies steel-silver,
    Would chamfer away
A knot in the grain of a streaming light, the glitter
    Off lances' points, that moved
A sluggish Froissart to aesthetic feeling.

And will the poet, carpenter of light,
    Work with the grain henceforward?
If glitterings won't fetch him
    Nor the refractory crystal,
Will he never again look into the source of light
    Aquiline, but fly
Always out of the sun, unseen till softly alighting?

Why, by an ingrained habit, elevate
    Into the light of ideas
The colourful trades, if not like Icarus
    To climb the beam? High lights
Are always white, but this ideal sun
    Dyes only more intensely, and we find
Enough cross-graining in the most abstract nature.

A Lily at Noon

Deep-sea frost, and
Lilies at noon . . .
Late leaves, late leaves
Toss every day.
The daymoon shines always for some.
In the marriage of a slow man
Eighteen years is soon.

Sun and moon, no
Dark between,
Foresight and hindsight
Halving the hours.
And now he collects his thoughts
Before it is too late.
But what can 'too late' mean?

Shielding with hands,
Binding to stakes . . .
Late leaves, late leaves
Toss every day,
The sun moves on from noon.
To freeze, to cup, to retard –
These measures terror takes.

Homage to John L. Stephens

There has to be a hero who is not
A predator but South
Of the Border down
Mexico way or wherever else she
Whispers, It's best not to linger.

Fever: bright starlight, and the sails
Flapping against the mast, the ocean
Glass, and the coastline dark,
Irregular, and portentous with volcanoes;
The Great Bear almost upon him, the North Star
Lower than ever, waning as he was waning,

And not that sort of hero, not
Conquistador Aeneas, but a tourist!
Uncoverer of the Maya, John L. Stephens,
Blest after all those beaks and prows and horses.

July, 1964

I smell a smell of death.
Roethke, who died last year
with whom I drank in London,
wrote the book I am reading;
a friend, of a firm mind,
has died or is dying now,
a telegram informs me;
the wife of a neighbour died
in three quick months of cancer.

Love and art I practise;
they seem to be worth no more
and no less than they were.
The firm mind practised neither.
It practised charity
vocationally and
yet for the most part truly.
Roethke, who practised both,
was slack in his art by the end.

The practice of an art
is to convert all terms
into the terms of art.
By the end of the third stanza
death is a smell no longer;
it is a problem of style.
A man who ought to know me
wrote in a review
my emotional life was meagre.

January

Arable acres heave
Mud and a few bare trees
Behind St Michael's
Kirby le Soken, where
The pew I share
Promises the vicinity I leave.

Diatribe and
Denunciation, where
I spend my days,
Populous townships, sink
Into the haze that lowers
Over my neighbours' land.

Resignation, oh winter tree
At peace, at peace . . .
Read it what way you will,
A wish that fathers. In a field between
The Sokens, Thorpe and Kirby, stands
A bare Epiphany.

Ezra Pound in Pisa

Excellence is sparse.
I am made of a Japanese mind
Concerning excellence:
However sparred or fierce
The furzy elements,
Let them be but few
And spaciously dispersed,
And excellence appears.

Not beauty. As for beauty,
That is a special thing.
Excellence is what
A man who treads a path
In a prison-yard might string
Together, day by day,
From straws blown in his path
And bits of remembering.

Sun moves, and the shadow moves,
In spare and excellent order;
I too would once repair
Most afternoons to a pierced
Shadow on gravelly ground,
Write at a flaked green-painted
Table, and scrape my chair
As sun and shade moved round.

Or, Solitude

A farm boy lost in the snow
Rides his good horse, Madrone,
Through Iowan snows for ever
And is called 'alone'.

Because gone from the land
Are the boys who knew it best
Or best expressed it, gone
To Boston or Out West,

And the breed of the horse Madrone,
With its bronco strain, is strange
To the broken sod of Iowa
That used to be its range,

The metaphysicality
Of poetry, how I need it!
And yet it was for years
What I refused to credit.

Pentecost

Up and down stairs of the inner ear,
Its ivory chambers, stray
The stumbling, the moving voices;
The self-communers; of whom
It seems hardly to matter
Whether we say that they are
Not at home in our language
Or they are too much at home.

What faculties we are lacking!
We have eyes to see, and we see
Not, sometimes; ears to hear and
Sometimes we hear. But they have
Faculties without organs;
They see and hear with the thorax,
They are eloquent in pidgin.

Our sons and our daughters shall
Prophesy? That gift of tongues
To the Beat and post-Beat poets,
The illiterate apostles,
Is what, if I should cherish
Much or mourn my lack of
Or ape their stammerings,
I must betray myself.

Epistle. To Enrique Caracciolo Trejo

Essex

A shrunken world
Stares from my pages.
What a pellet the authentic is!
My world of poetry,
Enrique, is not large.
Day by day it is smaller.
These poems that you have
Given me, I might
Have made them English once.

Now they are inessential.
The English that I feel in
Fears the inauthentic
Which invades it on all sides
Mortally. The style may die of it,
Die of the fear of it,
Confounding authenticity with essence.

Death, an authentic subject,
Jaime Sabinès has
Dressed with the yew-trees of funereal trope.
It cannot be his fault
If the English that I feel in
Feels itself too poor
Spirited to plant a single cypress.
It is afraid of showing, at the grave-side,
Its incapacity to venerate
Life, or the going of it. These are deaths,
These qualms and horrors shade the ancestral ground.

Sabinès in another
Poem comes down
To the sound of pigeons on a neighbour's tiles,
A manifest of gladness.
Such a descent on clapping wings the English
Contrives to trust
No longer. My own garden
Crawls with a kind of obese
Pigeon from Belgium; they burst through cracking branches
Like frigate-birds.

Still in infested gardens
The year goes round,
A smiling landscape greets returning Spring.
To see what can be said for it, on what
Secure if shallow ground
Of feeling England stands

Unshaken for
Her measure to be taken
Has taken four bad years
Of my life here. And now
I know the ground:
Humiliation, corporate and private,
Not chastens but chastises
This English and this verse.

I cannot abide the new
Absurdities day by day,
The new adulterations.
I relish your condition,
Expatriate! though it be among
A people whose constricted idiom
Cannot embrace the poets you thought to bring them.

Cheshire

A lift to the spirit, when everything fell into place!
So that was what those ruined towers remained from:
Engine-houses, mills. Our Pennine crests
Had not been always mere unfettered space.

Not quite the crests, just under them. The high
Cloughs, I learned in the history-lesson, had
Belted the earliest mills, they had connived
With history then, then history passed them by.

His savage brunt and impetus, one survives it?
Finding it all unchanged and the windowless mill
Between Wincle and Congleton silent and staring, I found
The widow's weeds restorative and fit.

And Mr Auden, whom I never knew,
Is dead in Vienna. A post-industrial landscape
He celebrated often, and expounded
How it can bleakly solace. And that's true.

Essex

Names and things named don't match
Ever. This is not
A plethora of language,
But language's condition;

Sooner or later the whole
Cloth of the language peels off
As wallpaper peels from a wall,
However it 'hangs together'.

With Essex moreover the case is
Especially grievous: hope,
Disappointment, fatuous shocks
And surprises pattern the fabric.

Constable's country merits
Better than I can give it
Who have unfinished business
There, with my own failures.

Mandelstam, on Dante

I

Russian Jew, for you
    To re-think Dante, dissolve
Into fluids that four-square slab
    Of Christendom, meant a resolve

(So it must seem) to taunt
    And tempt the unsteadied Gentile,
As it might be me, to act
    In nettled Stalin's style.
Dangerous, those corrosives
    You handle. First and last
Powder the graven image!
    'Jew' means 'iconoclast'.

Can we believe the impulse
    Consciously suicidal?
Or was the play of mind
    Lordly, the interest idle?

2

About the skies, you went wrong somewhere. Let
Some nearer neighbour of theirs make the corrections.
For them it was easier, them the nine Olympic
Dantescan discuses, to clang directions!

You are not to be thought of apart from the life you lived
And what Life intends is at once to kill and caress
That thus the distress which beat in on your ears, on your eyes
And the sockets of your eyes, be Florentine.

Let us not then assign to you, no, let us not fit about your
Hollowed-out temples that bittersweet prickle, the laurel –
Better in your case if we should split your
Heart into blue and clamorous bits of ocean.

For when you died, having served out your time,
You in your time friend to all lifetime-livers,
Yes, there transpired a broader, a loftier chime
Sent from the skies in your entire chest's heavings.

3 (*Voronezh, 1937*)

'About the skies, I went wrong somewhere. Let
Some nearer neighbour of theirs make the corrections.
For you it was easier, you the nine Olympic
Dantescan discuses, to clang directions,
Be out of breath, get black and blue contusions . . .

But Thou, if Thou art not the heretofore's
Nothing-accomplishing hero, if Thou art bent
Standing over me now, wine-steward, to proffer the cup,
Pour me the strong wine, not the ephemeral ferment
To drink of, to pledge the vertiginous, towering, straight-up
Insane blue-azure's hand-to-hand engagement.

Dovecotes, black holes, starlings' nesting-boxes,
Blue of the bluest, case of the key at its keenest,
Ice of the heretofore, high ice! – ice of the Spring . . .
Clouds, look – the clouds, against soft collusions
    embattled . . .
Quiet now! Storm-clouds, see where they lead them out,
    bridled.'

4

Rhyme, you once said, only
　　Points it up, tags it, the blue
Cabinet-making of Heaven
　　And Earth, the elegant joints
All of them flush as given!

Symmetries in this blue
　　Cabinet, the small
Rooms of stanzas – in this
　　No woe, you said, but the happy
Chances of mathematics.

Clouds come and go like a French
　　Polisher's breath on walnut,
Protean, fluid . . . And you
　　A lordly squandering playboy!
No bequest but you blue it!

At home in the Empyrean . . .
　　Yes, but one joint had sprung
Long, long ago. The woe
　　Came, and was Florentine?
As well say: Galilean.

Portland

After Pasternak

Portland, the Isle of Portland – how I love
Not the place, its name! It is as if
These names were your name, and the cliff, the breaking
Of waves along a reach of tumbled stone
Were a configuration of your own
Firm slopes and curves – your clavicles, your shoulder.
A glimpse of that can set the hallway shaking.
And I am a night sky that is tired of shining,
Tired of its own hard brilliance, and I sink.

Tomorrow morning, grateful, I shall seem
Keen, but be less clear-headed than I think;
A brightness more than clarity will sail
Off lips that vapour formulations, make
Clear sound, full rhyme, and rational order take
Account of a dream, a sighing cry, a moan.

Like foam on all three sides at midnight lighting
Up, far off, a seaward jut of stone.

To Thom Gunn in Los Altos, California

Conquistador! Live dangerously, my Byron,
In this metropolis
Of Finistère. Drop off
The edge repeatedly, and come
Back to tell us! Dogs and cherry-trees
Are not your element, although
You like them well enough when, cast

Ashore and briefly beached, our Commodore,
You take a turn among them, your cigar
Fragrant along a sunny garden wall,
Home between voyages, with your aunts in Kent.

Home . . . Is that home? Is even Land's End 'home'?
You shrug and say we are mid-Atlantic people,
You and I. I'd say for you
The mid-Pacific rather: somewhere out
On the International Dateline, so far out
Midsummer Oregon and midwinter Chile
Are equidistant, and 'the slow
Pacific swell' you generate lifts and crunches
Under the opalescent high fog with as much
Patience in one hemisphere as the other,
An exhalation from the depths you sound to.

The plesiosaur! Your lead-line has gone down to
The Age of Reptiles, even as
Over your head the flying lizard
Sprung from its Lompoc silo, Vandenberg Airforce Base,
Tracks high across mid-ocean to its target.
Ignore it, though a tidal wave will rage
From where it plunges, flood Japan
And poison Asia. This is the pacific
Ocean, the peacemaker. Nothing rhymes with this
Lethal indifference that you plumbed to even
Once in a bath-house in Sonoma County.

This is the end of the world. At the end, at the edge
We live among those for whom
As is natural enough
The edge is the navel of earth, and the end, the beginning.
Hope springs not eternal nor everywhere – does it
Spring in Kent? For these our friends, however,
It springs, it springs. Have we a share in it?

This is the Garden of Eden, the serpent coiled
Inside it is sleepy, reposeful. It need not flex
A muscle to take us. What are we doing here?
What am I doing, I who am scared of edges?

Grudging Respect

As when a ruined face
Lifted among those crowding
For the young squire's largesse
Perceives him recognize
Her and she grabs, not for any
Languidly lofted penny
They scrabble for, but for his eyes
And pockets them, their clouding
That instant; and the abruptness
With which his obliging is checked,
His suddenly leaving the place . . .
Just so may a grudging respect
Be, from a despised one,
Not just better than none
At all, but sweeter than any.

Having No Ear

Having no ear, I hear
And do not hear the piano-tuner ping,
Ping, ping one string beneath me here, where I
Ping-ping one string of Caroline English to
Tell if Edward Taylor tells
The truth, or no.

Dear God, such gratitude
As I owe thee for giving, in default
Of a true ear or of true holiness,
This trained and special gift of knowing when
Religious poets speak themselves to God,
And when, to men.

The preternatural! I know it when
This perfect stranger – angel-artisan –
Knows how to edge our English Upright through
Approximations back to rectitude,
Wooing it back through quarter-tone
On quarter-tone, to true.

Mystical? I abjure the word, for if
Such faculty is known and recognized
As may tell sharp from flat, and both from true,
And I lack that capacity, why should I
Think Paradise by other light than day
Sparkled in Taylor's eye?

Death of a Voice

After Pasternak
and to him

1

Here is its mark left, thumbnail of enigma.
– It is late, you will sleep, come dawn you will try to read it.
And meanwhile to awaken the loved one, and to touch her
As you may do is given to no other.

How you have touched her! Though your lips were bronze
They touched her, as tragedians touch the stalls.
A kiss there was like summer, hung and hung
And only after that, your sound of thunder.

It drank, as birds drink; took till the senses swooned.
Long, long the stars flowed in from throat to lung.
Nightingales too, their eyes start, as by spasms
Drop by drop they wring night's arches dry.

2

Dawn will agitate the tapers,
Spark and propel house-martins to their mark.
Admonitory, in you dart:
Let life be always as bran-new as this.

Dawn, like a shot into the dark.
Bang, bang! – the wadding as it flies
Out of the rifle sees its spark go out.
Let life be always as bran-new as this.

Once more, outside – a puff of wind.
What night-long waited on us quivers.
With dawn came rain, and the rain shivers.
Let life be always as bran-new as this.

It is distinctly ludicrous!
Why should it bother with the man on guard?
It saw its own way in was barred.
Let life be always as bran-new as this.

Give us your orders, now, upon the drop
Of a handkerchief, the while you are still *seigneur*
While, for the while that we are at a loss,
The while, the while the spark's not blown upon!

3

In the unparented, insomniac
Damp and universal vast
A volley of groans breaks loose from standing posts,
And still the nightwind, self-aborted, idles.

And hard behind, in an unseeing scurry
Some slant drops fall. About a stretch of fencing
Damp branches quarrel with the pallid wind
Sharply. I quail. You, bone of their contention!

The Thirty-ninth Psalm, Adapted

I said to myself: 'That's enough.
Your life-style is no model.
Keep quiet about it, and while
you're about it, be less overt.'

I held my tongue, I said nothing;
no, not comfortable words.
'Writing-block', it's called;
very discomfiting.

Not that I had no feelings.
I was in a fever.
And while I seethed,
abruptly I found myself speaking:

'Lord, let me know my end,
and how long I have to live;
let me be sure
how long I have to live.

One-finger you poured me;
what does it matter to you
to know my age last birthday?
Nobody's life has purpose.

Something is casting a shadow
on everything we do;
and in that shadow nothing,
nothing at all, comes true.

(We make a million, maybe;
and who, not nobody but
who, gets to enjoy it?)

Now, what's left to be hoped for?
Hope has to be fixed on you.
Excuse me my comforting words
in a tabloid column for crazies.

I held my tongue, and also
I discontinued my journals.
(They accumulated; who
in any event would read them?)

Now give me a chance. I am
burned up enough at your pleasure.
It is all very well, we deserve it.
But shelved, not even with mothballs?

Hear my prayer, O Lord,
and please to consider my calling:
it commits me to squawking
and running off at the mouth.'

Sing Unto the Lord a New Song

Cheerfulness in lordly
leisure; and
holiness in thunder and high wind.

The lordly thunder
cleaves out flakes of fire.

The lightning uncovers the woods,
making the roe deer calve
untimely in the bracken.

It is the holiness thunders.

Do not ask for the storm to ease.
Spirits rise, the longer it goes on.
Imagine Him yawning, hear Him
crack His joints as He stretches,
magisterial!

Praise the Lord upon the harp,
sing to him on the damnable steel guitar!

God Saves the King

To the chief Chanters
upon the dumb Dove in far places:
    either your brows are knitted,
    or you whinny and smirk, such teasers,
    you take such pains.

Far the places
and you are in their hands
who feast on squabs.

But care for that other way
of being debonair:

the sauntering monarch's, David's,
whose vigorous warmth did variously impart
to wives and concubines, to chariot-wheels,
to realms and officers,

religious faith; that is,
light spareness, unconcern.

Vengeance is Mine, Saith the Lord

You that would bite the whole pie and
mell with the pack, yet pout yourself ill-used,

you have committed crimes
against the innocent for
no profit but self-promotion.
Mouse has a broken back by
the coarsest cheese in the larder.

The creaking scissors and the penman's knife,
derailed from their proper business, will do justice
in a *collage* of your cruelties.
                            'The children
wore their cagoules, but these were mortar-bombs.'

In the casinos most were vacuous, some
were fleshy and flaming, some profuse, some grasping,
far from Beirut.
                    Though I
address the mute, He hears, will testify.

Put Not Your Trust in Princes

Let them give up the ghost, then there is nothing but dust
left of their presumptions we were fools enough to trust.

Pin no more hopes on them, nor the promissory collective;
the light at that end of the tunnel is glass, the credit delusive.

    In the presence of the authorities we spent our days
    turning our caps in our hands, and the manful,
        inveigling phrase.

    We combed our sparse hair in the mornings (silvered,
    we observed).
    We regarded our consort sleeping, whom we had
        shabbily served.

They are lost among the histories, names of world-mastering
      heroes:
this, the peace-fixer; that, the cuckolded smith of Infernos.

Having the sceptre no more, no more the ambiguous terms
of an unbelieved spokesman parade them; their press-men
      too feed worms.

Their Rectitude Their Beauty

'The angels rejoice in
the excellencies of God;
the inferior creatures in
His goodness; sinners only
in His forgiveness.'

His polar oppositions;
the habitable zones,
His clemencies; and
His smiling divagations,
uncovenanted mercies,

who turned the hard rock into a standing water
and the flint-stone into a springing well.

The voice of joy and health is in the dwellings of the
    righteous;
my eyes are running with rheum
from looking for that health

in one who has stuck by
His testimonies;
who has delighted in
His regimen; who has run
the circuit of His requirements;
whose songs in the caravanserai
have been about His statutes,
not to deserve nor observe them
(having done neither) but
for the angelic reason:

their rectitude,
their beauty.

Except the Lord Build the House

A song of the degrees,
of the gradations,
the steps to the temple . . .

There is no need to insist;
it is enough to name them.

For Zion is a city
uniform in itself,
compact together.

Why are you so strenuous, my soul?
Vain to get up early,
to sit up late,
to bolt your bread in a hurry.

Short be your sleep and coarse your fare
in vain. The Lord shall turn
the key in the captivity of Zion,
and all go like a dream.

The grass grows over the ruins of Eblis,
nobody's hayfield;
you are loitering there, or studying
hard (you are a hard
loiterer) but no one
going by in the road calls out
'Good morning' or 'Good luck'.

No use of early rising:
as useless is thy watching.
No traveller bestows
a word of blessing on the grass,
nor minds it as he goes.

Climb the stair
manfully, and sing
a short song on each step of the stair.

It is not an arduous duty.
Eblis was hard, not Zion.

Master & Man

Proverbs 19.22

Chaste and kind . . . 'a pattern'
(Isaac and Rebecca)
'chaste and kind'. Such words!
What we have done to you
both long ago and lately . . .

For 'chaste', read 'pure'; for 'kind'
('The desire of a man is his kindness')
read, 'What is desired in a man
is loyalty.' Biddable man!

My lord, my liege lord, my dear
lord, what I desire is
my own and not your kindness.

A poor man is better than a liar,
dear my lord, suppose the
desire of a man is his kindness;

extended also
to the unthankful,
whose kindness is as a morning cloud
and as the early dew it goeth away,

milord.

The Ironist

'Sacred? or sacrosanct?
or sanctimonious, even?
Suppose you chose these topics
(which, you will say, chose you),
hoping to escape
the debilitating scope
of your kind in your time and place:

irony.'

It is Lord Haw-haw speaking;
it is Mephistopheles speaking,
the syphilitic; it is
Germany speaking.

A masterly ironist
of history knows
his subject inside out;
his dry wit drying out
a sop of sentiment from
the cerements of the West.

Lover of the mephitic,
of fog and stink,
his natural haunt the road by the chemicals plant,

his elegant strong suit
is tacit and total carnage:
the Devil's work, whose mark
(frivolity and distraction)
is on this page also

as on the best we can do.

The Nosegay

The roses of irony blossom
floridly on the trellis
of inexperience crossed with
a need for the fell and certain.

Seeing that irony is
the adolescent's defence,
'An end to irony!' means
death to most of our lyrics.

The objection to the God
of Islam and of Judah,
'He lacks a sense of humour',
means, He is not ironical,
He is not a lyrical God.

He does not come and go;
He is not glimpsed in gaps of
time. Alas, it is clear that
He claims to be omnipresent,
and had better be thus acknowledged.

He has His sense of fun
surely; He has even
(as we see it, who wait on deathbeds)
a mordant wit.

It is the bite of the wit
mauls our sense of humour.

Lyrists may proclaim their
intermittent visions;
ironists, their protective
clothing; but the surgeon

of Islam and of Judah
makes His incisions
justly, and He is not
deprecating about it.

Stepping along the Turl,
selecting a buttonhole
half mauve, half mustard-yellow,
what God and what men you malign!

If I Take the Wings of the Morning

taking off at dawn
to circle *ultima thule*,

threading the splendours between
ice and pearl cloud cover,

God is not only also
there, but signally there,

who made the heavens skilfully,
who made the great lights
with a strong hand and a strained-out arm,

who brought forth clouds from the end of the world
and sent forth lightnings with rain
and out of His treasuries high winds.

When those who keep us in prison
ask of us mirth in our hang-ups
with 'Sing us a song of Zion',
what can we sing or say
under the mourning willows
of a common suffering in
the river-meadows of Babel?

It is our lingo utters us, not we.
Our native tongue, our endowment,
determines what we can say.
And who endowed us?

Speak if you cannot sing.
Utter with appropriate shudders
the extremities of God's arctic
where all the rivers are frozen,

and how He tempers our exile
with an undeserved planting of willows.

Samuel Menashe

O Many Named Beloved
Listen to my praise
Various as the seasons
Different as the days
All my treasons cease
When I see your face

Sheen

Sun splinters
In water's skin
Quivers hundreds
Of lines to rim
One radiance
You within

Roads run forever
Under feet forever
Falling away
Yet, it may happen that you
Come to the same place again
Stay! You could not do
Anything more certain –
Here you can wait forever
And rejoice at your arrival

Someone Walked Over My Grave

The breath breaks a cold shuddered hollow
That instant, unbearably, I know
The beauty of this world

Those lips the young man my father
Found more fair than the bud of a rose
Now almost touched to dust – kiss that dust
You trod God of Life, God of the world

All my friends are homeless
They do not even have tents
Were I to seek a safe place
I would run nights lost
Ice pelting my face
Sent the wrong way
Whenever I ask –
Afraid to turn back,
Each escape the last

Lie down below trees
Be your own guest
Give yourself up . . .
Under this attentive pine
Take your time at noon
The planes will drone by soon

Shade

Branches spoke
This cupola
Whose leaf inlay
Keeps the sun at bay

Winter

For Derek Mahon

I am entrenched
Against the snow,
Visor lowered
To blunt its blow

I am where I go

April

It is the sun that makes us smile
It is the sun and spring has come
Soon it will reach Norway
Her wooden villages wet
Laughter in each rivulet

My angels are dark
They are slaves in the market
But I see how beautiful they are

Carnival

Faces flowing up the street
Faces glowing to the feast
Great is the god they greet
Face to face, feet to feet

Fire Dance

Must smiles subside in a sigh
And sobs underlie laughter
Shall we always leap high
With flames leaping after

Autumn

I walk outside the stone wall
Looking into the park at night
As armed trees frisk a windfall
Down paths that lampposts light

Transfusion

Death awaited
In this room
Takes its time
I stand by
Your deathbed
Making it mine

The Moment of Your Death

My head bounces away
In the trough of a wave
You are unbound on your bed
Like water far from a shore
Nothing can reach you now
Not my kiss, not a sound
You are out of hearing
And I have run aground
Where gravel grinds
The face it blinds

The Bare Tree

My mother once said to me, 'When one sees the tree in leaf, one thinks the beauty of the tree is in its leaves, and then one sees the bare tree.'

1

Now dry stone holds
Your hopeful head
Your wise brown eyes
And precise nose

Your mouth is dead

2

The silence is vast
I am still and wander
Keeping you in mind
There is never enough
Time to know another

3

Root of my soul
Split the stone
Which holds you –
Be overthrown
Tomb I own

4

Darkness stored
Becomes a star
At whose core
You, dead, are

5

I will make you a landscape
Spread forth as waves run

After your death I live
Become a flying fish

The Offering

Flowers, not bread
Cast upon the water –
The dead outlast
Whatever we offer

My Mother's Grave

Bones
Are mortar
For your wall

Jerusalem

Dust
Upholds
Your street

The Oracle

Feet east
Head west
Arms spread
North and south
He lies in bed
Intersected
At the mouth

The friends of my father
Stand like gnarled trees
Yet in their eyes I see
Spring's crinkled leaf

And thus, although one dies
With nothing to bequeath
Enough love survives
To make us grieve

Memento Mori

This skull instructs
Me now to probe
The socket bone
Around my eyes
To test the nose
Bone underlies
To hold my breath
To make no bones
About the dead

Self Employed

For John Smith

Piling up the years
I awake in one place
And find the same face
Or counting the time
Since my parents died –
Certain less is left
Than was spent –
I am employed
Every morning
Whose ore I coin
Without knowing
How to join
Lid to coffer
Pillar to groin –
Each day hinges
On the same offer

November

Now sing to tarnish and good weathering
A praise of wrinkles which sustain us
Savory as apples whose heaps in attics
Keep many alive through old winter wars

The room of my friend
Is a violet chapel
Where in pale state he lies
And daydreams dapple
His blue eyes

Warrior Wisdom

Do not scrutinize
A secret wound –
Avert your eyes –
Nothing's to be done
Where darkness lies
No light can come

The Dead of Winter

In my coat I sit
At the window sill
Wintering with snow
That did not melt
It fell long ago
At night, by stealth
I was where I am
When the snow began

In My Digs

Caked in a glass
That is clear
Yesterday's dregs
Tell me the past
Happened here

Old Mirror

In this glass oval
As love's own lake
I face myself, your son
Who looks like you –
Once we were two

Sunset, Central Park

A wall of windows
Ignited by the sun
Burns in one column
Of fire on the lake
Night follows day
As embers break

Tenement Spring

Blue month of May, make us
Light as laundry on lines
Wind we do not see, mind us
Early in the morning

Windows: Old Widow

There is a pillow
On the window sill –
Her elbow room –
In the twin window
Enclosed by a grill
Plants in pots bloom
On the window sill

Enlightenment

He walked in awe
In awe of light
At nightfall, not at dawn
Whatever he saw
Receding from sight
In the sky's afterglow
Was what he wanted
To see, to know

66

She who saw the moon last night
She who swayed with the chant
Died in her sleep or dreams –
To say she is dead seems scant.

Full Fathom Five

Each new death opens
Old graves and digs
My own grave deeper
The dead, unbound, rise
Wave after wave
I dive for pearls
That were his eyes
But touch bedrock –
Not a coral reef –
Where my father lies
I come to grief

Nightfall

Eye this sky
With the mind's eye
Where no light fades
Between the lines
You read at night
Binding that text
Which days divide

Morning

I wake and the sky
Is there, intact
The paper is white
The ink is black
My charmed life
Harms no one –
No wife, no son

On the Level

In the sky's eye test
Does this desk, level
With the window sill,
Uphold my level best
Or is the bed better
For dreams that distil
Words to the letter

Curriculum Vitae

1

Scribe out of work
At a loss for words
Not his to begin with,
The man life passed by
Stands at the window
Biding his time

2

Time and again
And now once more
I climb these stairs
Unlock this door –
No name where I live
Alone in my lair
With one bone to pick
And no time to spare

Infant, Old Man

Up in arms
That hold her high
Enough to bend
Her father's ear
She babbles by
Me on a bench
At my wits' end.

Forever and a Day

No more than that
Dead cat shall I
Escape the corpse
I kept in shape
For the day off
Immortals take

Off the Wall

Broken mirror off the wall
All of a piece with the past
Whose splinters glint like glass
Stuck in the sole of my shoe –
If I'm out of luck
And down at the heel too
Are seven years enough
Time for me to do?

Family Silver

That spoon fell out
Of my mother's mouth
Before I was born,
But I was endowed
With a tuning fork

Improvidence

Owe, do not own
What you can borrow
Live on each loan
Forget tomorrow
Why not be in debt
To one who can give
You whatever you need
It is good to abet
Another's good deed

Night Music
(Pizzicato)

Why am I so fond
Of the double bass
Of bull frogs
(Or do I hear the prongs
Of a tuning fork,
Not a bull fiddle)
Responding –
In perfect accord –
To one another
Across this pond
How does each frog know
He is not his brother
Which frog to follow
Who was his mother
(Or is it a jew's harp
I hear in the dark)?

Red Glints in Black Hair

It is the rose below white
Gold suns under sea green
A nose formed for insight
Things visible but unseen
Keeping my eyes to the king
As I call wise night my queen

At Cross Purposes

1

Is this writing mine
Whose name is this
Did I underline
What I was to miss?

2

An upheaval of leaves
Enlightens the tree
Rooted it receives
Gusts on a spree

3

Beauty makes me sad
Makes me grieve
I see what I must leave

4

Scaffold, gallows
Do whose will
Who hallows wood
To build, kill

5

Blind man, anvil
No hammer strikes
Your eyes are spikes

Pity us
By the sea
On the sands
So briefly

On My Birthday

I swam in the sea our mother
Naked as the day I was born
Still fit at forty-four
Willing to live forever

Salt and Pepper

For Calvin Bedient

Here and there
White hairs appear
On my chest –
Age seasons me
Gives me zest –
I am a sage
In the making
Sprinkled, shaking

Using the window ledge
As a shelf for books
Does them good –
Bindings are belts
To be undone,
Let the wind come –
Hard covers melt,
Welcome the sun –
An airing is enough
To spring the lines
Which type confines,
But for pages uncut
Rain is a must.

The Sandpiper

The sandpiper
Scampers over sand
Advances, withdraws
As breakers disband

Each wave undergoes
The bead of his eye
He pecks what it tows
Keeps himself dry

Night Watch

The heart I hear in bed tonight
Is mine – it frightens me
To hear my heart so clearly
It could stop at any time

Keep your ear to the ground
I was told without fear
Now I am hollowed for sound
And it is my heart I hear

At Millay's Grave

Your ashes
In an urn
Buried here
Make me burn
For dear life
My candle
At one end –
Night outlasts
Wick and wax
Foe and friend

At a Standstill

That statue, that cast
Of my solitude
Has found its niche
In this kitchen
Where I do not eat
Where the bathtub stands
Upon cat feet –
I did not advance
I cannot retreat

Le Lac Secret

For Paul Keegan

They have now traced me to my uncles
One died a beggar in a room with no windows
And one danced until he was undone, like Don Juan
Though they try to find me out, I am still as the swan
While those who search grow grim
And darker in their doubt

Sleep
gives wood its grain
Dreams knot the wood

     *   *   *

The hollow of morning
Holds my soul still
As water in a jar

     *   *   *

A pot poured out
Fulfills its spout

     *   *   *

The sea staves
Concave waves

     *   *   *

O Lady lonely as a stone
Even here moss has grown

Take any man
Walking on a road
Alone in his coat
He is a world
No one knows
And to himself
Unknown

Yet, when he wanders most
It is his own way, certain
As spheres astronomers note
In their familiar motion

Telescoped

The dead preside
In the mind's eye
Whose lens time bends
For us to see them
As we see the light
Shed by dead stars
Telescopes enlarge

Waterfall

Water falls
Apart in air
Hangs like hair
Light installs
Itself in strands
Of water falling
The cliff stands

Twilight

Looking across
The water we are
Startled by a star –
It is not dark yet
The sun has just set

Looking across
The water we are
Alone as that star
That startled us,
And as far

Just now

With my head down
Bent to this pen
Which is my plow
I did not see
That little cloud
Above the field –
Unfurrowed brow,
You are its yield

Gray Boulder

Gray boulder
Beside the road
You devote me to age
Whose date none decodes
From signs of fire or ice –
Elephant among field mice
You crouched here alone
In the silence of stone

Dominion

Stare at the sea
you on your chair
sinking in sand,
Command the waves
to stand like cliffs,
Lift up your hand

Dreaming

Windswept
as the sea
at whose ebb
I fell asleep,
dreams collect
in the shell
that is left,
perfecting it.

Awakening from Dreams

Flung inside out
The crammed mouth
Whose meal I am
Ground, devoured
I find myself now
Benignly empowered

Reeds Rise from Water

rippling under my eyes
Bullrushes tuft the shore

At every instant I expect
what is hidden everywhere

Manna

Open your mouth
To feed that flesh
Your teeth have bled
Tongue us out
Bone by bone
Do not allow
Man to be fed
By bread alone

'And He afflicted thee and suffered thee to hunger and fed
thee with manna, which thou knewest not neither did thy
fathers know; that He might make thee know that man does
not live by bread alone, but by every word that proceeds from
the mouth of the Lord does man live.'

– Deuteronomy VIII:3

Paschal Wilderness

Blue funnels the sun
Each unhewn stone
Every derelict stem
Engenders Jerusalem

Promised Land

At the edge
Of a world
Beyond my eyes
Beautiful
I know Exile
Is always
Green with hope –
The river
We cannot cross
Flows forever

As the tall, turbaned
Black, incense man
Passed the house
I called after him
And ran out to the street
Where at once we smiled
Seeing one another
And without a word
Like a sword that leaps from its lustrous sheath
He was swinging his lamp with abundant grace
To my head and to my heart and to my feet . . .
Self-imparted we swayed
Possessed by that One
Only the living praise

'The dead do not praise Thee.'

                                          – Psalm of David

If I were as lean as I feel
Only my bones would show
Living bone, ideal –
Without a shadow –
For the exacting dance
That the Law commands
Until I overstepped
The forbidden ark
To take on flesh
Wrestling in the dark

The Niche

The niche narrows
Hones one thin
Until his bones
Disclose him

The shrine whose shape I am
Has a fringe of fire
Flames skirt my skin

There is no Jerusalem but this
Breathed in flesh by shameless love
Built high upon the tides of blood
I believe the Prophets and Blake
And like David I bless myself
With all my might

I know many hills were holy once
But now in the level lands to live
Zion ground down must become marrow
Thus in my bones I am the King's son
And through death's domain I go
Making my own procession

Old as the Hills

The lilt of a slope
Under the city
Flow of the land
With streets in tow
Where houses stand
Row upon row

Night Walk

For John Thornton

In eyes of strangers glimpsed
On the street at night
I see more than meets the eye
In the broad daylight

The circumspect passer-by
Keeps to himself, and yet
His eyes give him the lie
At once when they are met

Dusk

night
into
earth
from
rise
Voices

Rural Sunrise

Furrows erupt
Like spokes of a wheel
From the hub of the sun —
The field is overrun —
No rut lies fallow
As shadows yield
Plow and bucket
Cart and barrow

A flock of little boats
Tethered to the shore
Drifts in still water
Prows dip, nibbling

In Stride

Streets at night like decks
With spars overhead
Whose rigging ropes
Stars into scope

Pirate

For P.N. Furbank

Like a cliff
My brow hangs over
The cave of my eyes
My nose is the prow of a ship

I plunder the world

Dreams

What wires lay bare
For this short circuit
Which makes filaments flare –
Can any bulb resist
Sockets whose threads twist
As fast as they are spun –
Who conducts these visits
Swifter than an eclipse
When the moon is overcome?

Awakening

Like one born again
To the same mother
I wake each morning
The same, another
Who takes my name
But cannot place me
In dreams, nightmares
Where I became
The one she bears

I lie in snows
Drifted so high
No one knows
Where I lie

April (Fool)

Stars I leap
Clearing a puddle
Why was I deep
In a muddle?

Sudden Shadow

Crow I scorn you
Caw everywhere
You'll not subdue
This blue air

To Open

Spokes slide
Upon a pole
Inside
The parasol

Infanta

Below, between
Her dam and her sire
She stands alone
In grown-up attire

Cargo

Old wounds leave good hollows
Where one who goes can hold
Himself in ghostly embraces
Of former powers and graces
Whose domain no strife mars –
I am made whole by my scars
For whatever now displaces
Follows all that once was
And without loss stows
Me into my own spaces

Voyage

Water opens without end
At the bow of a ship
Rising to descend
Away from it

Days become one
I am who I was

Downpour

Windowed I observe
The waning snow
As rain unearths
That raw clay —
Adam's afterbirth —
No one escapes
I lie down, immerse
Myself in sleep
The windows weep

Adam Means Earth[*]

I am the man
Whose name is mud
But what's in a name
To shame one who knows
Mud does not stain
Clay he's made of
Dust Adam became —
The dust he was —
Was he his name

[*] From *Adamah*, 'earth' in Hebrew.

Simon Says

In a doorway
Staring at rain
Simple withstands
Time on his hands

Scissors

Sharpen your wit –
Each half of it –
Before you shut
Scissors to cut

Shear skin deep
Underneath wool
Expose the sheep
Whose leg you pull

Home Movie

Awake at once
No space between
The day and dream
Seen as it runs
Me off the screen
No time to splice
Slices of life –
I'm wide awake,
No second take.

The scrutiny
Of a chicken's eye
Terrifies me –
What does it think?
Not brain but beak
Chills my blood –
It stares to kill

What to Expect

At death's door
The end in sight
Is life, not death
Each breath you take
Is breathtaking

Save your breath
Does not apply –
You must die.

Sparrow
For Naomi Lewis

That busy body darts
Under the pigeon to filch
A crumb bigger than his bill
Beggar, thief, get what you can

He's no song bird –
Chirps one note –
There is a pearl
Stuck in his throat

A Bronze Head

He's in his garden now
Sticking his neck out
Of a flower bed,
A head without shoulders

We are not statues yet
Nor about to become
Immortals, thoroughbreds
At the starting post
Programmed to run
A race against ghosts
Whose inside track
Stakes out the hindmost
For us, taken aback
By the prowess we lack.

The Spright of Delight

For Kathleen Raine

The spright of delight
Springs, summersaults
Vaults out of sight
Rising, self-spun
Weight overcome

Transplant

I would give
My liver, kidneys
Heart itself
For you to live
In perfect health
With me, your clone
Whose grafted cells
Grow marrow, bone

If all else fails
Do not reject
My skin or nails
Whatever's left
Of me for you
By a hair's breadth
Will see us through

Peace

As I lie on the rock
With my eyes closed
Absorbed by the sun
A creak of oarlocks
Comes into the cove

Hallelujah

Eyes open to praise
The play of light
Upon the ceiling –
While still abed raise
The roof this morning
Rejoice as you please
Your Maker who made
This day while you slept,
Who gives grace and ease,
Whose promise is kept.

'Let them sing for joy upon their beds.'
– Psalm 149

A-
round
my neck
an amu-
let
Be-
tween
my eyes
a star
A
ring
in my
nose
and a
gold
chain
to
Keep me
where
You
are
*

Allen Curnow

Narita

Turning its eyes from side to side, inquiring
brightly, the head of the worm issues
from the door for arrivals.

The door for departures is where papers are
handed in. There are many of these,
all numbered. Never look back.

Between the two the meantime is all there is.
It passes of itself. Your cabin
crew girls are for off-duty

fantasies. Abaft the loo the tail section
ruptures, the sky inhales heavily,
a change of plan is announced,

all four hundred, some gifted or beautiful
or with greedy heirs, have to die now,
only to make sure of you

this instant sooner or later than you think.
The prettiest accessories, like
silk scarf, matching lipstick, badge

of rank are brightness fallen from the air, you
will never see it. The uniformed
personnel most pitiably

heaped, colours of daedal feathers, the smells of
burning, a ring'd finger, a baby's
foot bagged for the mortuary.

No, you will never see it. Wish yourself then
the best of Lucifer's luck. This indoors
world's roof is geodetic,

as good as any heaven, and better lit
than the broad daylight it simulates,
out of hearing of the rising

and the falling scream and sight of the nearest
numbered gate. Picture to yourself some
small green hills with ginkgo trees.

Gare SNCF Garavan

The day doesn't come to the boil, it guards
A banked-up flame under a cool first light.
Madame tethers her Siamese to the doorway
of the Gare SNCF, the shadier side
of the tracks where we mustn't stray.

The tracks are bare, the pines don't stir, the haze
is international, Cap Martin is a thing
in the mind's eye of 'that eternal sea',
Bordighera just one more. Behind the doorway
of the sanctuary, something rings, Madame is

answering. I am questioning a blossom of
some nameless yellow creeper about the excitements
of life on a warm wall. Pussy is overweight,
so is Madame, but active, panties and *collants*
hang from an upper room, over the yard side

of the Gare, the seaward, shaded by the dark
eyelashes of the pines in a light that is not
explicit. Landward the Alpes Maritimes lean
scarily steep-to, by the Gare clock
I can relax, nobody's yet begun saying

'to the mountains, fall on us', only indistinct
voices drop from the lemon-gardens, the villas.
A frequent service. Madame emerges, bearing her
official baton, producing a train from Nice,
Italy's minutes away, an old-fashioned thought,

an old-fashioned iron expostulation of
wheels, fluttering doors, interrupts nothing.
So much at risk, a miracle that so much gets
taken care of, Madame picks up her cat from
the *quai* and cuddles it, conversing with friends.

Menton, London
1983

Do Not Touch the Exhibits

A gulp of sea air, the train
bites off a beach, re-enters the rock.
A window, a blind cathode, greyly reflects,
Plato sits opposite, his nose in a map.
Where you're going's never what you see

and what you saw, is that where you went?
Is there a reef with an angler on it
whose rod makes a twitching U?
Has he landed his fat silver-gilt
dorado, smack! on a pan in the mind?

Why can't I cut corners and have them?
Daylight chips in again, with cypresses,
olives, loquat (*nespola* the Japan
medlar, not the one you eat rotten,
the other sort, butter-yellow, sweet

embedding slippery outsize pips),
artichokes, the native littoral
cultivations, rivermouth litter,
punctured cans, plastic bottles,
and behind (supposedly) the weatherish

pink and chrome villas gingerly
seated, shutters to seaward,
the Ligurian blue, too much of it.
Or weathering the long cape
another fisherman whose limping

boat I'm overhauling? a file
of red and white Martini sunbrollies
wheels in, peels off, drops back.
A brace of NATO frigates present
unmuzzled guns, 'optional extras'.

Beachcombings, introjections,
best stuffing for tunnels. Venus
on her lee-shore *poco mosso*
paroled from the Uffizi, screwed
to the wall under the baggage rack,

space reserved in the mind, goes
where I go, my side of the glass
beneath which our family motto's pinned,
è pericoloso sporgersi
indelibly incised on steel.

Rapallo, London
1983

A Reliable Service

The world can end any time
it likes, say, 10.50 a.m.
of a bright winter Saturday,

that's when the *Bay Belle*
casts off, the diesels are picking
up step, the boatmaster leans

to the wheel, the white water
shoves Paihia jetty back.
Nobody aboard but the two of us.

Fifteen minutes to Russell
was once upon a time
before, say, 10.50 a.m.

The ketch slogging seaward
off Kororàreka Point,
the ensign arrested in

mid-flap, are printed and
pinned on a wall at the end
of the world. No lunch

over there either, the place
at the beach is closed. The *Bay
Belle* is painted bright

blue from stem to stern.
She lifts attentively. That
will be all, I suppose.

A Balanced Bait in Handy Pellet Form

Fluent in all the languages dead or living,
the sun comes up with a word of worlds all spinning
in a world of words, the way the mountain answers
to its name and that's the east and the sea *das Meer,*
la mer, il mare Pacifico, and I am on my way to school

barefoot in frost beside the metalled road
which is beside the railway beside the water-race,
all spinning into the sun and all exorbitantly
expecting the one and identical, the concentric,
as the road, the rail, the water, and the bare feet run

eccentric to each other. Torlesse, no less,
first mountain capable of ice, joined the pursuit,
at its own pace revolved in a wintry blue
foot over summit, snow on each sunlit syllable,
taught speechless world-word word-world's A B C.

Because light is manifest by what it lights,
ladder-fern, fingernail, the dracophyllums
have these differing opacities, translucencies;
mown grass diversely parched is a skinned 'soul'
which the sun sloughed; similarly the spectral purples

perplexing the drab of the dugover topsoil
explain themselves too well to be understood.
There's no warmth here. The heart pulsates
to a tune of its own, and if unisons happen
how does anybody know? Dead snails

have left shells, trails, baffled epigraphy
and excreta of such slow short lives,
cut shorter by the pellets I 'scatter freely',
quick acting, eccentric to exorbitant flourishes
of shells, pencillings, drab or sunlit things

dead as you please, or as the other poet says,
Our life is a false nature 'tis not in
the harmony of things. There we go again, worrying
the concentric, the one and identical, to the bone
that's none of ours, eccentric to each other.

Millions die miserably never before their time.
The news comes late. Compassion sings to itself.
I read the excreta of all species, I write
a world as good as its word, active ingredient
30 g/kg (3%) Metaldehyde, in the form of a pellet.

Canst Thou Draw Out Leviathan with an Hook?

I

An old Green River knife had to be scraped
of blood rust, scales, the dulled edge scrubbed
with a stone to the decisive whisper of steel
on the lips of the wooden grip.

You now have a cloud in your hand
hung blue dark over the waves and edgewise
luminous, made fast by the two brass rivets
keeping body and blade together, leaving
the other thumb free for feeling
how the belly will be slit and the spine severed.

The big kahawai had to swim close
to the rocks which kicked at the waves
which kept on coming steeply steaming,
wave overhanging wave
in a strong to gale offshore wind.

The rocks kicked angrily, the rocks
hurt only themselves, the seas without a scratch
made out to be storming and shattering,
but it was all an act that they ever broke
into breakers or even secretively
raged like the rocks, the wreckage of the land,
the vertigo, the self-lacerating
hurt of the land.
                         Swimming closer
the kahawai drew down the steely cloud
and the lure, the line you cast
from cathedral rock, the thoughtful death
whispering to the thoughtless,

Will you be caught?

II

Never let them die of the air,
pick up your knife and drive it
through the gills with a twist,
let the blood run fast,
quick bleeding makes best eating.

III

An insult in the form of an apology
is the human answer to the inhuman
which rears up green roars down white,
and to the fish which is fearless:

if anyone knows a better it is a man
willing to abstain from his next breath,
who will not be found fishing from these rocks
but likeliest fished from the rip,

white belly to wetsuit black, swung copular
under the winching chopper's bubble,
too late for vomiting salt but fluent at last
in the languages of the sea.

IV

A rockpool catches the blood,
so that in a red cloud of itself
the kahawai lies white belly uppermost.

Scales will glue themselves to the rusting blade
of a cloud hand-uppermost in the rockpool.

V

Fingers and gobstick tail,
the hook's fast in the gullet,
the barb's behind the root
of the tongue and the tight
fibre is tearing the mouth
and you're caught, mate, you're caught,
the harder you pull it
the worse it hurts, and it makes
no sense whatever in the air
or the seas or the rocks
how you kick or cry, or sleeplessly
dream as you drown.

A big one! a big one!

In the Duomo

I

Recitative

This is the rock where you cast your barbed wishes.
    That is the clifftop where you hang by the eyes.
    Here is where Leviathan lives.

It is all in the walls of one great shell incised.
    The instructions look simple, the trouble is the smoky
    ambiguous morning sunlight, the heights inside

the cathedral are blurred. So much for art, which only
    comprehends the introversions of arches,
    lunettes, capitals, where the sunlight slowly

floats up towards their rock-hung perches
    motes moths wings claws human hands fluttering
    prayers kites clapping gustily to barefoot beaches,

the tidiness of a carved by time discoloured
    eminence being magnetic to such poor untidy
    littles or nothings,

bits and pieces, yet 'of such' is the highly
    esteemed 'kingdom of heaven', what else?
    Imagine an enormous face, conceive it smiling

to an accompaniment of birds and bells
    down blurred clifftops, makebelieve masonry,
    by interior sunlight extinguished at eye level

which is rock bottom. Here the linens, the sacred
    silverware are arranged and the blood is poured
    by experienced hands which do not shake

serving up to Messer Domineddio god and lord
    the recycled eternity of his butchered son,
    this mouthful of himself alive and warm.

This is homoousianus, this is the cup
    to catch and keep him in, this is where he floats
    in a red cloud of himself, this is morning sun

blotting the columns, the ogives, the hollowed throne,
    smoking the kite-high concavity of the cliff.
    This is the question, *Caught any fish?*
                                        Say, *No.*

I am teaching Leviathan to swim.

II

A Professional Soldier

Ma ficca li occhi a valle chè s'approccia
    la riviera del sangue, in la qual bolle
    qual che per violenza in altrui noccia

That's every one of us, man and woman and child.
    We all boil together when we boil
    up to our necks in the river so ardently imagined

(*Inferno* canto twelve lines 46–48),
    merely to exist being even for the gentlest
    the rape of another's breath or bread.

Gian-Battista Montesecco's problem was believing
    everything he read, the divinest poets
    told the sublimest lies, common sense was as rare

then as now, and that no such river existed
    for stewing damned humanity was much too big
    and flat a contradiction for this hired soldier,

throats cut, cities pillaged, assassinations,
　　　no job too small, go anywhere. His theology
　　　was eschatology, death judgment heaven hell,

he put last things first where they belong.
　　　There's life to be got through yet eternity's only
　　　a matter of time a hell of a long time.

Killer without qualms, he never forgot his basics,
　　　they scared the daylights out of Montesecco
　　　as nothing on earth could do, to do him justice.

III

A Turning Point in History

It had to be an offering acceptable
to God, for which good reason, and for others
of a practical nature they decided the cathedral
was the place, and the time High Mass.

The flood of a king tide, the deepest sounding
where the big ones are, the holiest lure,
the tackle secure, the steel and the stone
scraped crosswise in *hoc signo*, can you beat it?

Where the pavement is cold underfoot
and over it full flow, high blood, High Mass
brings purple and princelier scarlet
scuffing the sea floor, graining the green,

and the other poor fish and the drab
discolorations of plankton, il popolo del dio
threadbare in Tuscan shoddy, miraculous draught
in the visible and invisible nets.

Hot hand for the gold, he got cold feet,
Montesecco did. He told this fat cat Pazzi,
I'll do you a fair day's kill for a fair day's pay,
but the banquet's where we settled for, am I right?

You keep your side of it, I'll keep mine,
I'll dagger you a dozen Medici at anybody's table
except Christ's. Two will be sufficient, Pazzi said.
Who's paying? And Montesecco, Who's going to burn?

You can stuff the whole deal and to hell with the money
where it comes from. There's an Englishman down there
eternally boiling for chilling his man at Mass,
when they lifted up the Host he stuck in the steel.

A crick in the neck isn't the worst you get
staring at the judgment in the roof of San Giovanni
and the damned people the size of a skinned eel
in Beelzebub's teeth and the fire from Christ's left foot.

And you're caught, mate, you're caught!

I'll take my chance of the pit, Ser Jacopo,
but I'm waiting till I'm pushed if it's all the same,
I'm not jumping. To which Pazzi, What if I tell you
this is for Rome, the holy father himself

blesses the act? Not on for double the money,
Montesecco said. And might as logically say
another half chiliad later than this latest
photographer studying for Bonechi's *Guide*

Ghiberti's regilded doors of paradise
and the godsize Jesus dooming in the dome,
not counting the time eternity takes one day
mopping up the bloody mess on the floor below.

IV

26 April 1478

So they had to find somebody else
whose numinous nightmares
didn't unman his mind for the day's
churchmanlike chores,

whose mortal infirmities,
profane daydreams, dirt
in the ears and the nose, the involuntary
or surreptitious fart,

lascivious leakages,
the sea-cock under the cope,
were the daily wick, wax, oil and soot,
the smell of the shop,
for whom agnus and sursum corda
and gloria in excelsis,
candles on the lips, made light
of the darkest policies.

Pazzi found two priests
for the cathedral job,
Volterra's Antonio Maffei,
apostolic scribe,
Stefano curate of Montemurlo;
putting first things first,
whichever were last, they judged
the time right for murder.

Ite missa est.
The rite being said and done,
in a scarlet stir the hit-men edged
each to his man.
Lorenzo dropped his shoulder
quicker than Maffei struck
his fumbled blow and the blood ran down
from the nicked neck.

Blood fell, the rumpus rose
under the haughty summits
from the fractured glassy sea
to the mistiest limits,

and where was the other priest?
Stefano got no closer
than a dagger's draw from the mark
at the *ite missa*,

and the two young Cavalcanti
joined Il Magnifico,
and they knifed it out in the sacristy
to save Lorenzo,
leaving his brother dead
where he had to die
face down, by the Pazzi's jabbing steel
dancing wasp time.

Giuliano de' Medici
bled where he had to bleed,
bedrock flat on the church floor
in the cloud he made
of the strong bestial smell
of dissolving clay,
their offering to the oldest god
that holiest day.

V

An Old Hand

I tried from the cathedral
    yesterday and had no luck,
        Mrs Dragicevic said.

Slaty grey strata
    angled and squared abutted
        the clubfoot of the cliff

where she perched, this plump
    vigilant bird, in her blue
        quilted parka, pointing her

4.0 m. fibreglass pole
    over each big wave that walked
        white from the west

with a long bearded howl,
    broke roaring into a run
        for the rocks to come.

And the spot was a good one,
    the cathedral, so long as you kept
        your head for heights

and the big ones came,
    il magnifico and his brothers
        to the turn of the tide,

having to, having to come
    leaping to the holy lure,
        an acceptable offering

to the blooding hand, the scaling,
    the scarlet clouded pool,
        the necessary knife.

Dichtung und Wahrheit

A man I know wrote a book about a man he knew
and this man, or so he the man I know said, fucked
and murdered a girl to save her from the others
who would have fucked and murdered this girl
much more painfully and without finer feelings,
for letting the Resistance down and herself be fucked
by officers of the army of occupation, an oblation
sweet-smelling to Mars and equally to porn god Priapus.

What a fucking shame, this man the one the man
I know knew decided, if you want a job done well
do it yourself, and he did and he left her in a bath
of blood from the hole in her neck which he carved
in soldierly fashion, a way we have in the commandos,
after the fuck he knew she didn't of course
was her last, and a far far better thing, wasn't it?
than the bloody fuckup it would have been if he'd left her
to be unzipped and jack-the-rippered by a bunch
of scabby patriots with no regimental pride.

And he had this idea, and he mopped up the mess
and he laid her out naked on a bed with a crucifix
round her neck for those bastards the others
the sods to find, furious it must have made them.

And the man I know who knew this man or some other
man who did never forgot this fucking story,
it wouldn't leave him alone till he'd shown this goon
who actually did or said he did or was said to have done
the fucking deed what a better educated man
would have done and thought in his place.
And he wrote this book.

Experience like that, he exclaimed,
thrown away on a semiliterate whose English
was so imperfect you could hardly be certain
that what he did and what he said were connected,
let alone, by no fault of his own,
ignorant of the literature on the subject.
What can you do, with nothing but a cock
and a knife and a cuntful of cognac,
if you haven't got the talent?

A big one!

After Dinner

Arnold Wall 1869–1966

At ninety he told the press,
I suppose you are going to ask me
how I manage to live so long,
and so well.
    Five years later,
facing me across his table,
having lifted the glass of red
wine to an untremulous
lip, and set it down
with a steady hand, he remarked
that he once possessed the whole
of the *Comédie humaine*
in a Paris edition. Couldn't
remember now what became of it.

Between him and his death's
left foot the gangrene was
no secret, already in the door
and pressing hard, in a white fold freshly
dressed for dinner.
                          Other whitenesses
were summits, mountain faces,
alps both Southern and Swiss,

Tibet, one icy toehold
after another, still climbing now
in the thinnest air, the last
of all those ups and downs.

Having read many books, taught some,
and written a few, after dinner
announced, as it were, a decision,
I have been here long enough.

A little after that, Lawrence?
D. H. Lawrence? Terrible young man.
Ran away with my friend Weekley's wife.

All true, as it happened. Twice
the mortifying foot, from under the table
published his pang, the grimace no sooner
read than cancelled, very civilly.

Blind Man's Holiday

I

Is the word 'adult'? Utamaro's engulfing
vulvas, deep thought! Füssli's girls muscling in, a
moist-handled glans, *shockingly indelicate,*

poor wretch! Flaxman said, *looking ineffably
modest*, one didn't blame the widow Füssli's
thrift, who stoked the kitchen range with them, making

sea-coal burn bluer. Was less at stake for Bruno
in Venice, incinerated, ineffably
for something ineffable? Ashes, in the end.

Stuff your pillow-book with metaphysics for
the best bedside read, it takes the place of what
takes place, pictures or *pensées*, the same thing.

The picture in the mind revives, our poet
noticed, and so do I. These agreeable
sensations moved over and made room for *sad*

perplexity, and back again, having once
orbited the earth. I re-enter, entering
you. The mind's too full of itself, to make sense

of Pascal or the creed of Saint Athanasius
damp and hot from the press, 'would you believe it?'
What does God smell of but the dust of hassocks,

wine, laundered linen, a creation of Patou
fingertipped behind the ears? Angel surrogates
shinny up and down the fire-escape, flapping

at bedroom and bathroom windows, all fingers
and feathers. She's too full and he's too busy to
notice much, only *gleams of half-extinguished*

thought, in the light of what takes place, no other
light really than these, which take the place of it.
A particular darkness forgets our visits.

II

What happened? What's happening? Somebody drew
a funny face on a big shell, BANG! you're dead
all of you, Ol' Bill ducks his helmet, it flies

past grinning, or bounces off a parapet.
In a serious oil-painting nobody gets
obscenely eviscerated, the war artist's

a dab hand at cosmetic bandaging, he
patches up with white, with a fine tip adds red
for the head-wounds, mostly in the scalp and brow,

the eyes of the wounded are forget-me-not
blue, gun-flashes vermilion, virginal pink
for the faces, like begonia blooms in shit

which is khaki *dunnest smoke*, old-masterly
murk *that my keen knife see not the wound it makes
nor Heaven peep through.* Heaven does. One painted

star blinks benignly. A child in the sun sees
it all in The Queen's Gift Book where Adam hides
because he is naked. My bank manager's

choice is a framed cauliflower cloud, the atoll
vertically blown up out of a silk-screen
ocean. Glass catches the light. Entering, I

turn it to the wall, unwilling to pre-empt
the untriggered fact, the picture in the mind,
the job in hand. Its relevance is obscure.

What's pain time? Your long wire, Alvin Lucier, sings
to the oscillator, end over end, glistens
in your darkened gallery. This is our midnight
ride in a wet gale banging the heads of the trees

together. Quartz watches don't keep it, humane
quackery knows what's quickest for capital
offenders, mortal inhalation, 'lethal
injection', make up your mind, how would you like

to die? In a flash, a puff, *an unconscionable
time a-dying* the king said or was said to have
said? Duration is public, the intensity
private, God's wink, a lifetime, a million years.

Where are we now? Between gulps of gas, that's twice
I've asked, this time he answers Saint Luke's, meaning
the supermarket not the church, I grunt back
gratefully, meaning neither, the hospital's

any minute now by pain time, a quick fix could
conveniently snap the wire, drop the dumb ends
in a puddle of terminal quiet, no
more random glistenings, no sound-images

whipped off the street. I want it stopped. Where are we?
The ambulance corners with a shrug, straightens,
windshield wipers egg-scramble headlights, greens, reds,
ambers, unquantifiable messes of wet

incandescences. Squatting, he holds the gas
bottle as steadily as he can. I lie
still too. The driver's shoulder's a dark function.
It's an 'essential service' we all perform,

Monday is beginning, Sunday's casualties
unloading still, full as a party balloon

with pain the mind bobs unserviceably while
somebody is brought in dead. I want my shot

and a couple of 50 mg
indocid is all I'm getting if that's true
about the key to the cupboard where they keep
the morphine and the sister who comes on duty

at five, that's four hours more of this, the
bloody sheet keeps slipping off. You get the picture?
Amnesia, muse of deletions, cancellations
revives, revises pain, a ride in the dark.

I. The packets of Utamaro postcards any traveller can buy at a Japanese
airport contain no examples of the eighteenth-century master's erotic
art; nor do historians (I suppose) connect this genre peculiarly with the
name of his Western contemporary Henry Fuseli, the adoptive name,
that is, of the Swiss-born Johann Heinrich Füssli. It is a somewhat
circumscribed modern taste which discovers them both in, say, some
production of the Erotic Art Book Society – in company with Rem-
brandt, Rowlandson, Grosz, Balthus, Dali, and Picasso. Does anybody
know whether Sacheverell Sitwell guessed correctly that 'hundreds of
these exceptionable drawings may have escaped Mrs Fuseli's kitchen-
range'? Or how deeply scandalized friends like Flaxman and Haydon
actually were, learning of their existence at the time of the artist's
death in 1825? My source is Eudo C. Mason, *The Mind of Henry Fuseli*
(London, 1951), citing Benjamin Haydon's *Diary* and Allan Cun-
ningham's *Life* of Fuseli. II. A First World War early childhood left a
few of Bairnsfather's popular cartoons of trench warfare sharply printed
on my memory. *The Queen's Gift Book* would be one of those sumptu-
ously got-up volumes published under royal patronage in aid of patri-
otic funds; there were cosmetic paintings of scenes at the Front, like
the retreat from Mons, in the lurid colour reproduction of the time.
III. Alvin Lucier's 'long wire' was on loan to the Auckland City Art
Gallery for a time in 1984, a wonderful contrivance, not only for the
electronically translated sounds intended by the American composer,
but visually as well. Voices or footsteps in the gallery, noises in the street
outside, made a continuously changing murmur about almost every-
thing. Not mere 'electro-acoustic natural photography', as someone
described Luc Ferrari's *Daybreak on the Beach*: much nearer, even painfully,
to one's sole self. – 1986

Jack-in-the-Boat

is always ready to row across the bath or lake.
Wind up the motor, and watch him dip his
blades like a true oarsman – in, out, in, out –
with never-tiring enthusiasm.

      – legend on a toy-maker's package

Children, children, come and look
Through the crack in the corner of the middle of the world
At the clockwork man in a cardboard house.
He's crying, children, crying.
He's not true, really.

Once he was new like you, you see
Through the crack in the corner of the middle of the night,
The bright blue man on the wind-up sea,
Oh, he went so beautifully.
He's not true, really.

Oh cruel was the pleasure-land they never should have
    painted
On the front and the back, the funny brand of weather,
For the crack in the corner of the middle of the picture
Let the colours leak away.
He's not true, really.

One at a time, children, come and look
Through the crack in the corner of the middle of the day
At Jack-in-the-Boat where the light leaves float.
He's dying of a broken spring.
He's not true, really.

A Sight for Sore Eyes

They wrap mountains round my eyes,
they say 'look' and it's all what they say
where the colour, that's another word is
deepest blue, and that's the colour of
the wind, blowing this way, warm and dry
coming from the mountains, visibly.

I have eyes in the back of my neck
too, the sun is mumbling the day's news
over my head. In so many words.
My morning bath was warm, out of a tap.
This garden is just one year younger
than I, 'girdled round' five years ago

with six-foot galvanised iron on
rimu posts, the sawn timber elsewhere
supports the Number 8 fencing wire
with one barbed strand, a little rusted.
The new vicarage is a 'bungalow',
the veranda faces north by west,

casements are fashionable magic
again, since the double-hung sash went
out, opening on the forms of pain, of
mumbled words, mountainously pronounced.
Too small to see over, I can thread
my 'line of vision' through a nail-hole

in the iron. I give it a tug.
The mountains have shifted at their moorings,
shudder and heave clear. The biggest wind's
in that quarter, it loosens the snows,
the Green Road is under water, old
Mr and Mrs Troon in a boat

are 'taken out' repeated in a dream
of the Troons, the Troons! What have I done?
What are the Troons doing 'taken out'
in a boat in the dark up Green Road,
old and ugly and wet? The wind was
never so dry and warm or the smell

of sheep so sour or the dust so thick
in the macrocarpas. The mountains
are the colour of wind, the highway
north is a pillar of dust by day
half-blinding riders and dogs, westward
the river still rises. My mother

bathes my eyes with boracic, she ties
up torn dianthus, delphinium, phlox
wasted on the alluvium the storm-
waters have been scraping seaward since
the sun mumbled the first implanted
word. My mother grows it all from seed.

A Raised Voice

Let it be Sunday and the alp-high
summer gale gusting to fifty miles.

Windmills groan in disbelief, the giant
in the pulpit enjoys his own credible

scale, stands twelve feet 'clothed in fine linen'
visibly white from the waist up, all

inferior parts masked, as my father
ascends three steps, is cupped like an egg.

The pulpit floor's eye-level, I look
up, Gordon Brown looks up, my father

looks down at his notes and begins in the
name of the father and of the son

and of the holy ghost amen, a voice
that says Jess to my mother, heightened

three steps, to which add the sanctuary
rise, the subdued pile of the Axminster

runner. Panels of a pale-coloured wood
liturgically pointed assemble

to enclose and to elevate the voice:
is it soft *kahikatea*, so readily

riddled by the worm of the borer
beetle but ideal for butter-boxes

or heart *kauri*? the rape of the northern
bush left plenty for pulpits and pews.

Gordon Brown, grocery and general store,
before kneeling always pushes one

oily vessel up clear of his head, the
tin lampshade clashes, the pulley squeaks.

I'm looking up into my thought
of my father, my certainty, he'll

be safe, but what about me? What else?
A voice descends, feet scrape, we all

stand up. The scent my mother wears is
vera violetta. That can't be it.

An Evening Light

The sun on its way down torched the clouds and left
them to burn themselves out on the ground:

the north-west wind and the sun both drop at once
behind the mountains. The foreground fills

with a fallen light which lies about the true
colours of absconded things, among

which I place this child whose tenth birthday happens
to have been my father's, that will be

a hundred years next Thursday. We were to meet
at a time of precisely such radiant

discolorations, the city of his mind.
The smallest leaf's alight where he looks

at the riverside willows, the painted iron
glows cold where he holds the garden gate.

The butcher's horse drops golden turds which steam
in sundown chill, an old man minds where

he walks, whose viridescent black assigns him
to an age before the city was,

I take his (my father's) hand: we follow him,
bowler hat, silver-topped stick, the hand

knuckled into the small of his back, which aches
to think of riding wet to the girths

and stirrups cutting up a country the size
of England with a sackful of pegs.

Under the one fallen firelit sky the Ngai-tahu
kainga and excavated *paa*

mark time by moa-bone middens, oceanic
migrations. What gospel will my father

preach to Tuahiwi, counting communicants
and the collection? A lamp-post cab-horse

blows into its nosebag, the old man fumbles
at his fob, his gold Waterbury's right

by the Post Office clock. By this light the city
is instant history, my father's mind.

The Ngai-tahu tribe occupied, and still claim, a great part of the South
Island of New Zealand. A *kainga* is a Maori settlement, a *paa* was a
fortified (stockaded) place or stronghold. In common European speech,
paa is often used for any form of Maori settlement; infrequently and
locally, *kainga* is heard in the corrupt form 'kaik'. – 1989

Survivors

Night falls on an unusual scene of public
rejoicing. A whole head taller than the crowd,

astride my father's nape, I can see the *jets
d'eau* the fire brigade pumps across the lake,

ebulliently spouted, illuminated.
Rose-coloured spectaculars blown to waterdrops

float off briskly, lifted into the dark
as the land-breeze variably puffs. Up above

searchlights find nothing but weather and themselves
(a dustier glare is where I see those headlamps

juddering for ever and all the way home
and hear the motor fire steadily) because

it's the end of the war, these are survivors
by the long wash of Australasian seas

a diminuendo of bells, guns, and prayers and
all these people simply enjoying themselves.

A wind freshens across the park, the crowd begins
thinning towards tomorrow. Climb up and see.

A Time of Day

A small charge for admission. Believers only.
Who present their tickets where a five-
barred farm gate gapes on its chain

and will file on to the thinly grassed paddock.
Out of afternoon pearl-dipped light the
dung-green biplane descended

and will return later, and later, late as
already it is. We are all born
of cloud again, in a caul

of linen lashed to the air-frame of the age,
smelling of the scorched raw castor oil
nine whirling cylinders pelt

up-country-smelling senses with, narcotic
joyrides, these helmeted barnstormers
heavier scented than hay,

harnesses, horsepiss, fleeces, phosphates and milk
under the fingernails. I'm pulling at
my father's hand *Would the little*

boy for selling the tickets? One helmet smiles
bending over yes, please yes let me,
my father hesitates, I

pull and I don't let go. Neither does the soul
of the world, whatever that is, lose
hold of the load, the bare blue

mountains and things hauled into the time of day
up that steep sky deepening from sea-
level all the way west again,

this paddock, the weight of everything, these people
waiting to be saved, without whom there's
no show, stay in place for ever.

A hand under each arm I'm held, I'm lifted
up and over and into an open
cockpit *Contact!* Gnome-LeRhône

fires ninefold, the chocks kicked clear, my balaclava
knits old sweat and foul oil, where tomorrow
was encloses me now.

The Pug-mill

At his age, he must know what it is
to have hands of clay and a child looking on.
A life by dug-out light under the hillside,
he has copied so often the one

thought baked in the bones of his wrist, there's
no obvious excuse for stopping now, so long
as there's a next there's no last. I am this child.
I watch Mr Prisk raise his left hand

eye-level (his own) as high as where
a bit of unweeded green light leaks beneath
a punky window-sash and pull on the rope's
knotted end. Up above in the sun

his horse hears the bell and stumbles out
of a doze into the collar and begins
orbiting the pug-mill, plods a muddy zodiac
which in its turn turns. Clotted clay buries

the workbench again. With palping palms
he stuffs his mould, that's one more circle squared, one
more brick the desert will keep. A contribution.
Its damp six faces sparkle dully

because of the sand which helps them slide
out whole into the system we inhabit here.
Is there anything outside? The hillside steepens
till baffled it stops, this way by blue

air that way by blue water, a third
which escapes between I'm running barefoot home
Corsair Bay, Flea Beach, pines of the town Domain
past the burned-out house with one dead brick

chimney standing. They are asking *Where-
ever have you been?* I tell them *Helping Mr Prisk.*

A Touch of the Hand

Look down the slope of the pavement
a couple of kilometres, to where it empties
its eyeful of the phantoms of passers-by

into mid-morning light which tops it up again
with downtown shadows. There has to be a city
down there and there is, and an 'arm of the sea',

a cloud to sprinkle the pavement, a wind
to toss your hair, otherwise your free hand
wouldn't brush it from your eyes, a welcome

touch of sincerity. As they pass down hill
away from you, their backs, and uphill towards you
their faces, the ages, the sexes, the ways

they are dressed, even one 'smile of recognition',
beg an assurance the malice of your mind
withholds. Look down, confess it's you or they:

so empty your eye and fill it again, with
the light, the shadow, the cloud, the other city,
the innocence of this being that it's the malice

of your mind must be the ingredient making
you possible, and the touch which brushes
the hair from your eyes on the slope of the pavement.

The Weather in Tohunga Crescent

It becomes 'unnaturally' calm
the moment you wonder who's going
to be first to ask what's happened
to the wind when did we last see

or watch for it animate the
bunched long-bladed heads
of the *ti* tree and all the dials
fidget in the sky and then it did

and we breathed again? The moment
comes when the bay at the bottom
of the street has been glassy a moment
too long the wind is in a bag

with drowned kittens god knows
when that was and which of us
will be first to say funny what's happened?
And it won't be a silly question

when it's your turn in the usual
chair to stare up into the cloud-cover
in which a single gull steeply
stalling dead-centred the hole

in a zero the stillest abeyance
and vanished into the morning's
expressionless waterface
'not a line on paper' your finger

pricks as if it might but won't
be lifted for something say switch
off the 'life support system' of the
whole damned visible material

world quite calmly would that be
fair to the neighbours or the birds
other ideas? Seven oystercatchers
at a standstill a study in black

and red beaks all the better to
stab with are modelling for Audubon
mounted on sand in the frame of your
own choice with nothing to shift

the cloud around the morning could
easily be dead mirror to mouth
not the foggiest hope fluttering
the wind-surfer lies flat on the beach

failing actual wind a pressure from
that quarter north-east as it happens
and another pressure like time
squeezes the isthmus the world you

didn't switch off so that coolly
as you recline bare-armed looking
up the spongy firmament has begun
drizzling the paper's getting wet

put the pen down go indoors
the wind bloweth as it listeth or listeth
not there's evidently something
up there and the thing is the spirit

whistle for it wait for it
one moment the one that's one too
many is the glassiest calm an
'intimate question' for the asking.

The Vespiary: A Fable

Its thoughts are modular, they attach themselves
to the young tree, the soffit of the back porch,
a grey box with multiple apertures where

its visible business is with legs and wings
purposefully hesitant, the unseen venom
is contingent, the sting for later inquiry.

I write. Those writings which we now identify
doubtfully as such yield nothing. I transcribe
tapes of the period recovered from pack ice,

leaning hard on the crude systems in use today.
I construe gaps, blips, ambiguous phonemes
and learn that the day after the first confirmed

sightings country children were sent home early
from school, a pet goat found stung dead on its tether.
Townspeople who'd never heard of honey dew

ran out into the streets, crying and silent.
Unopposed meanwhile, our oceanic nation's
defences in traditional disrepair,

the feral Vespoidea victory in their grasp
thrust inland, seized ornamental trees, PVC
downpipes breeches of abandoned guns ditched

cars, open mouths, armpits, natural nests
of which the naturalness has taken centuries
issuing the safe side of history's mirror.

I write. The past itself encoded itself
known only to itself and is dead, and we
live in our different style. No one knows how

many millions perished while our two species
achieved symbiosis by selection, between
this beach and that mountain 'under Capricorn',

in an agon of orifices, host and guest,
legs, wings, damp secretions. Now the dark swarms, my
lips mumble words over the busy bodies.

I write. The bones of the last boatpeople from
the north and the west lay somewhere under the dunes
where dogs dug and we played. When I was a kid

that's what we said. The safest thing's to touch nothing
on the beach, the back of the cave, the riverbed,
never leave the nest in the bush, where you were born

and suckled. A mother's cry stings me in my
mind's ear stuck to the tape, another tongue trapped
in the dead of time, *Attention! les guêpes!*

Things to Do with Moonlight

I

Holy Week already and the moon
still gibbous, cutting it fine
for the full before Jesus rises,
and imaginably gold
and swollen in the humid heaven.

First, second, and last quarters
dated and done with now,
the moon pulls a face, a profane
extemporisation,
gold gibbous and loose on the night.

Hot cross buns were never like this,
the paschal configurations
and prefigurations could never have
nailed the moon down
to the bloody triangle on the hill.

By the spillage of light the sea told
the cliff precisely where to mark
the smallest hour when I woke
and went out to piss
thankfully, and thought of Descartes,

most thoughtful and doubtful pisser,
who between that humid light
and the dark of his mind discerned
nothing but his thoughts
e. & o.e. as credible, and himself

because he thought them, his body
had a soul, his soul had a body,
an altogether different matter,
and that made two of him
very singularly plural, *ergo*

sum couldn't be *sumus*. He thought
deeply and came up with the solution
of blood in spirit, holy adhesive,
God, singular sum
best bond for body and soul.

II

And the height of the night being humid,
thickened with autumn starlight
to the needed density and the sea
grumbling in the west,
something visceral took the shape of an idea,

a numen, a psyche, a soul,
a self, a cogitation squirmed
squirmed, somebody standing there
broke wind like a man
whose mind was on other things.

His back to me and black
against the gibbous gold
of the godless moon, still blinking
the liturgical full,
something stuck its ground like a man

in a posture of pissing out of doors,
thankfully by moonlight, thinking
of pissing, experiencing the pleasure
and the pleasure of thinking
of pissing, hearing also the sea's

habitual grumble. Descartes?
I queried, knowing perfectly well it was.
And he to me, Your Karekare doppelgänger
travesties me no worse
than the bodily tissue I sloughed in Stockholm –

no wonder I caught my death
teaching snow queen Christine,
surely as her midnights outglittered
my sharpest certainties
an icicle must pierce my lungs

(at five one midwinter morning,
the hour she appointed for philosophy
by frozen sea, freezing porches)
and my zeroed extension
wait there for the awful joyful thaw.

There's the customary stone I'm sure,
with the customary lie incised,
the truth being I exist here thinking,
this mild March night.
As for the thought, you're welcome.

III

No less true it was I, meaning me,
not he that was physically present
pissing, and metaphysically
minding the sepulchre
not to be opened till after the full moon.

Cogito. I borrowed his knife
to cut my throat and thoughtfully
saw the blood soaking the singular
gold humid night.
Ergo sum. Having relieved myself

of that small matter on my mind,
I leaned lighter on my pillow
for a gibbous moon, a philosopher's
finger on his cock,
and a comfortable grumble of the sea.

'Karekare doppelgänger' names the place (Karekare) where the poem
was written, on the steeply forested coast of the Tasman Sea, west of
Auckland; I have spent most of my summers and weekends there since
1961. All four syllables are sounded, rather like English 'carry-carry'; a
native (or instructed) Maori speaker might give the vowels different
values, more like Italian, and stress the word differently.

The Parakeets at Karekare

The feathers and the colours cry
on a high note which ricochets
off the monologue of the morning sun
the long winded sea, off Paratohi posturing
on a scene waiting to be painted.

Scarlet is a squawk, the green
yelps, yellow is the tightest cord
near snapping, the one high note, a sweet-sour
music not for listening. The end is
less than a step and a wink

away as the parakeet flies.
Darkness and a kind of silence under
the cliff cuts the performance,
a moment's mixture. Can scavenging
memory help itself?

What do I imagine coloured words
are for, and simple grammatical
realities like, 'I am walking to the beach'
and 'I have no idea what the sky can mean
'by a twist of windy cloud'?

What's the distance between us all
as the rosella cries its tricolour
ricochet, the tacit cliff, Paratohi
Rock in bullbacked seas, my walking eye
and a twist of windy cloud?

The Loop in Lone Kauri Road

By the same road to the same
sea, in the same two minds,
to run the last mile blind or
save it for later. These
are not alternatives.

So difficult to concentrate! a powerful
breath to blow the sea back
and a powerful hand to haul it
in, without overbalancing.
Scolded for inattention,

depending on the wind, I know
a *rimu* from a *rewarewa*
by the leaf not 'coarsely serrate',
observant of the road roping
seaward in the rain forest.

A studied performance, the way
I direct my eyes, position
my head, 'look interested'.
Fine crystal, the man said,
you can tell by the weight,

the colour, the texture. The dog
steadies, places a healthy turd
on the exact spot. We like it
in the sun, it keeps our backs
warm, the watertables

dribble down the raw red cutting
the road binds, injured natures are
perfect in themselves. We liked it
at the movies when they nuked the city,
and suspended our disbelief

in doomsday, helping out the movie.
NEW YORK STATE jogs past me,
ribcage under the t-shirt stacked
with software, heart-muscle programmed
for the once round trip,

crosses my mind, by the bridge
at the bottom, the road over which
and the stream underneath are thoughts
quickly dismissed, as we double
back, pacing ourselves.

Concentrate! the hawk lifts off
heavily with an offal of silence.
Forget that, and how the helicopter
clapper-clawed the sea, fire-bucketing
the forest, the nested flame.

You Will Know When You Get There

Nobody comes up from the sea as late as this
in the day and the season, and nobody else goes down

the last steep kilometre, wet-metalled where
a shower passed shredding the light which keeps

pouring out of its tank in the sky, through summits,
trees, vapours thickening and thinning. Too

credibly by half celestial, the dammed
reservoir up there keeps emptying while the light lasts

over the sea, where it 'gathers the gold against
it'. The light is bits of crushed rock randomly

glinting underfoot, wetted by the short
shower, and down you go and so in its way does

the sun which gets there first. Boys, two of them,
turn campfirelit faces, a hesitancy to speak

is a hesitancy of the earth rolling back and away
behind this man going down to the sea with a bag

to pick mussels, having an arrangement with the tide,
the ocean to be shallowed three point seven metres,

one hour's light to be left and there's the excrescent
moon sponging off the last of it. A door

slams, a heavy wave, a door, the sea-floor shudders.
Down you go alone, so late, into the surge-black fissure.

Lo These Are Parts of His Ways

and to make up my mind about God before
he makes up his about me put myself
in Wallace Stevens's place and
God wherever he pleases
and a precious pair of us that makes

two minds in two minds each about
the other or say four deadlines
in search of a Last Supper
r.s.v.p. time running out
no entry on the diary's blank last

fly life's dateless day
numinous yesses and noes making
minds up alters nothing materially
can you see God changing his or
being in more than one about

anybody's finally settling
for 'naturally' the right one like
in the event of malfunction aborting
the count-down? our recreation's
chess he's white and I'm black

the board expands infinitely
at an infinite speed like Pascal's point
with mirrors which mirror mirrors
behind each of us his lips think
in his native Russian one forefinger

pauses on a pawn's or a bishop's
bonnet when it lifts we both know
that move's for keeps operations
belong to control where celestial
software lisps eternal

zero zeroes to the pacemaker
aorta *soft drum* the screen's bare
of digits all circuits locked *prepare to
meet thy God* have you an appointment?
belief hung in mid-mind between

the ethereal and the dustiest
answers let it hang! whose creature
whose creator to believe him into
existence or out of it? the heart
grows obsolete bottled protons

of an irrefutable *might
majesty dominion and power* poke
infernal noses into heavenly
business mutually assured
destruction keeps both of us guessing

demonstrable changes in the forms
of matter like fire-storms hanging
fire *Et O ces voix*
d'enfants chantant DIES IRAE
DIES ILLA exist in a mirror

a lifted forefinger for God's sake
whose? playing for keeps
my playmate's one unbelievably small
particle and who knows whose dust's
on fire in whose mind's eye?

Continuum

The moon rolls over the roof and falls behind
my house, and the moon does neither of these things,
I am talking about myself.

It's not possible to get off to sleep or
the subject or the planet, nor to think thoughts.
Better barefoot it out the front

door and lean from the porch across the privets
and the palms into the washed-out creation,
a dark place with two particular

bright clouds dusted (query) by the moon, one's mine
the other's an adversary, which may depend
on the wind, or something.

A long moment stretches, the next one is not
on time. Not unaccountably the chill of
the planking underfoot rises

in the throat, for its part the night sky empties
the whole of its contents down. Turn on a bare
heel, close the door behind

on the author, cringing demiurge, who picks up
his litter and his tools and paces me back
to bed, stealthily in step.

A Dead Lamb

Never turn your back on the sea.
The mumble of the fall of time is continuous.

A billion billion broken waves deliver
a coloured glass globe at your feet, intact.

You say it is a Japanese fisherman's float.
It is a Japanese fisherman's float.

A king tide, a five o'clock low, is perfect
for picking mussels, picking at your ankle-bones.

The wind snaps at the yellow-scummed sea-froth,
so that an evanescence of irised bubbles occurs.

Simply, silverly the waves walk towards you.
A ship has changed position on the horizon.

The dog lifts a leg against a grass-clump
on a dune, for the count of three, wetting the sand.

There is standing room and much to be thankful for
in the present. Look, a dead lamb on the beach.

Acknowledgements

The poems in this selection are taken from the following books, to whose publishers acknowledgement is made: *Brides of Reason* (Fantasy Press, Oxford, 1955), *A Winter Talent* (Routledge, 1957), *New and Selected Poems* (Wesleyan, 1961), *Events and Wisdoms* (Routledge, 1964), *Essex Poems* (Routledge, 1969), *Collected Poems 1950–1970* (Routledge, 1972), *The Shires* (Routledge, 1974), *In the Stopping Train* (Carcanet, 1977), *Three for Water Music* (Carcanet, 1981), *To Scorch or Freeze* (Carcanet, 1988) and *Collected Poems 1971–1983* (Carcanet, 1990) for Donald Davie; *The Many Named Beloved* (Gollancz, 1961), *No Jerusalem But This* (October House, 1971), *Fringe of Fire* (Gollancz, 1973), *To Open* (Viking, 1974) and *Collected Poems* (National Poetry Foundation, 1986) for Samuel Menashe; *Poems 1949–1957* (Mermaid Press, Wellington, 1957), *Trees, Effigies, Moving Objects* (Catspaw Press, Wellington, 1972), *An Incorrigible Music* (Auckland University Press/Oxford University Press, 1979), *You Will Know When You Get There* (Auckland University Press/Oxford University Press, 1982), *The Loop in Lone Kauri Road* (Auckland University Press/Oxford University Press, 1986), *Continuum: New and Later Poems* (Auckland University Press, 1989) and *Selected Poems 1940–1989* Viking/Penguin, 1990) for Allen Curnow.